SAFETY SYMBOLS

SAFETY SYMBOLS	HAZARD	EXAMPLES	PRECAUTION	REMEDY
DISPOSAL	Special disposal procedures need to be followed.	certain chemicals, living organisms	Do not dispose of these materials in the sink or trash can.	Dispose of wastes as directed by your teacher.
BIOLOGICAL	Organisms or other biological materials that might be harmful to humans	bacteria, fungi, blood, unpreserved tissues, plant materials	Avoid skin contact with these materials. Wear mask or gloves.	Notify your teacher if you suspect contact with material. Wash hands thoroughly.
EXTREME TEMPERATURE	Objects that can burn skin by being too cold or too hot	boiling liquids, hot plates, dry ice, liquid nitrogen	Use proper protection when handling.	Go to your teacher for first aid.
SHARP OBJECT	Use of tools or glassware that can easily puncture or slice skin	razor blades, pins, scalpels, pointed tools, dissecting probes, broken glass	Practice common-sense behavior and follow guidelines for use of the tool.	Go to your teacher for first aid.
FUME	Possible danger to respiratory tract from fumes	ammonia, acetone, nail polish remover, heated sulfur, moth balls	Make sure there is good ventilation. Never smell fumes directly. Wear a mask.	Leave foul area and notify your teacher immediately.
ELECTRICAL	Possible danger from electrical shock or burn	improper grounding, liquid spills, short circuits, exposed wires	Double-check setup with teacher. Check condition of wires and apparatus.	Do not attempt to fix electrical problems. Notify your teacher immediately.
IRRITANT	Substances that can irritate the skin or mucous membranes of the respiratory tract	pollen, moth balls, steel wool, fiberglass, potassium permanganate	Wear dust mask and gloves. Practice extra care when handling these materials.	Go to your teacher for first aid.
CHEMICAL	Chemicals that can react with and destroy tissue and other materials	bleaches such as hydrogen peroxide; acids such as sulfuric acid, hydrochloric acid; bases such as ammonia, sodium hydroxide	Wear goggles, gloves, and an apron.	Immediately flush the affected area with water and notify your teacher.
TOXIC	Substance may be poisonous if touched, inhaled, or swallowed	mercury, many metal compounds, iodine, poinsettia plant parts	Follow your teacher's instructions.	Always wash hands thoroughly after use. Go to your teacher for first aid.
OPEN FLAME	Open flame may ignite flammable chemicals, loose clothing, or hair	alcohol, kerosene, potassium permanganate, hair, clothing	Tie back hair. Avoid wearing loose clothing. Avoid open flames when using flammable chemicals. Be aware of locations of fire safety equipment.	Notify your teacher immediately. Use fire safety equipment if applicable.

Eye Safety Proper eye protection should be worn at all times by anyone performing or observing science activities.

Clothing Protection This symbol appears when substances could stain or burn clothing.

Animal Safety This symbol appears when safety of animals and students must be ensured.

Radioactivity This symbol appears when radioactive materials are used.

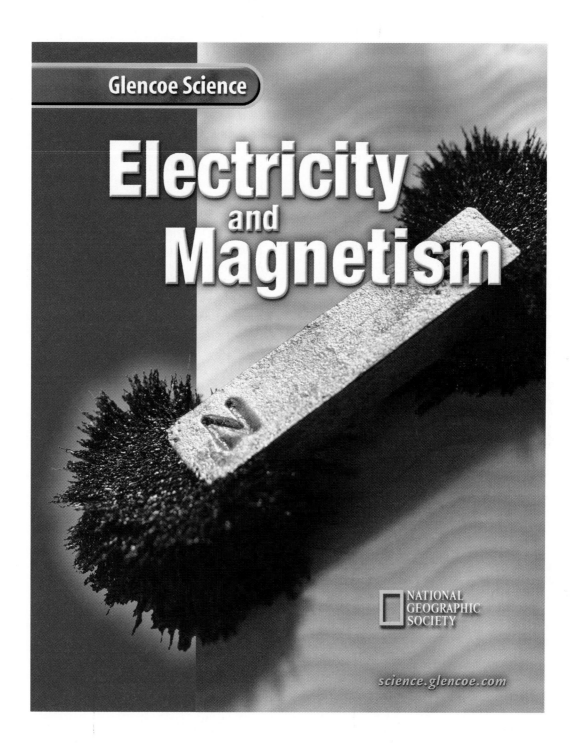

Glencoe Science

Electricity
and
Magnetism

NATIONAL GEOGRAPHIC SOCIETY

science.glencoe.com

Mc Graw Hill **Glencoe McGraw-Hill**

New York, New York   Columbus, Ohio   Woodland Hills, California   Peoria, Illinois

Glencoe Science

Electricity and Magnetism

Student Edition
Teacher Wraparound Edition
Interactive Teacher Edition CD-ROM
Interactive Lesson Planner CD-ROM
Lesson Plans
Content Outline for Teaching
Dinah Zike's Teaching Science with Foldables
Directed Reading for Content Mastery
Foldables: Reading and Study Skills
Assessment
    Chapter Review
    Chapter Tests
    ExamView Pro Test Bank Software
    Assessment Transparencies
    Performance Assessment in the Science Classroom
    The Princeton Review Standardized Test Practice Booklet
Directed Reading for Content Mastery in Spanish
Spanish Resources
English/Spanish Guided Reading Audio Program
Reinforcement

Enrichment
Activity Worksheets
Section Focus Transparencies
Teaching Transparencies
Laboratory Activities
Science Inquiry Labs
Critical Thinking/Problem Solving
Reading and Writing Skill Activities
Mathematics Skill Activities
Cultural Diversity
Laboratory Management and Safety in the Science Classroom
MindJogger Videoquizzes and Teacher Guide
Interactive CD-ROM with Presentation Builder
Vocabulary PuzzleMaker Software
Cooperative Learning in the Science Classroom
Environmental Issues in the Science Classroom
Home and Community Involvement
Using the Internet in the Science Classroom

THE PRINCETON REVIEW

"Study Tip," "Test-Taking Tip," and the "Test Practice" features in this book were written by The Princeton Review, the nation's leader in test preparation. Through its association with McGraw-Hill, The Princeton Review offers the best way to help students excel on standardized assessments.

The Princeton Review is not affiliated with Princeton University or Educational Testing Service.

Glencoe/McGraw-Hill

A Division of The McGraw-Hill Companies

Cover Images: Iron filings cluster around the north and south poles of a bar magnet.

Send all inquiries to:
Glencoe/McGraw-Hill
8787 Orion Place
Columbus, OH 43240

ISBN 0-07-825619-4
Printed in the United States of America.
3 4 5 6 7 8 9 10 027/111 06 05 04 03 02

Authors

National Geographic Society
Education Division
Washington, D.C.

Cathy Ezrailson, PhD
Science Department Head
Academy for Science and
Health Professions
Conroe, Texas

Dinah Zike
Educational Consultant
Dinah-Might Activities,
Inc.
San Antonio, Texas

Margaret K. Zorn
Science Writer
Yorktown, Virginia

Consultants

Content

Alan Bross, PhD
High-Energy Physicist
Fermilab
Batavia, Illinois

Jack Cooper
Adjunct Faculty Math and Science
Navarro College
Corsicana, Texas

Lee Meadows, PhD
UAB Education Department
Birmingham, Alabama

Carl Zorn, PhD
Staff Scientist
Jefferson Laboratory
Newport News, Virginia

Safety

Malcolm Cheney, PhD
OSHA Chemical Safety Officer
Hall High School
West Hartford, Connecticut

Sandra West, PhD
Associate Professor of Biology
Southwest Texas State University
San Marcos, Texas

Reading

Barry Barto
Special Education Teacher
John F. Kennedy Elementary
Manistee, Michigan

Rachel Swaters
Science Teacher
Rolla Middle School
Rolla, Missouri

Math

Michael Hopper, DEng
Manager of Aircraft Certification
Raytheon Company
Greenville, Texas

Reviewers

Anthony DiSipio
Octorana Middle School
Atglen, Pennsylvania

George Gabb
Great Bridge Middle School
Chesapeake, Virginia

Eddie K. Lindsay
Vansant Middle School
Buchanan County, Virginia

H. Keith Lucas
Stewart Middle School
Fort Defiance, Virginia

Series Activity Testers

José Luis Alvarez, PhD
Math/Science Mentor Teacher
El Paso, Texas

Nerma Coats Henderson
Science Teacher
Pickerington Jr. High School
Pickerington, Ohio

Mary Helen Mariscal-Cholka
Science Teacher
William D. Slider Middle School
El Paso, Texas

José Alberto Marquez
TEKS for Leaders Trainer
El Paso, Texas

Science Kit and Boreal Laboratories
Tonawanda, New York

CONTENTS

CHAPTER
3

Interdisciplinary Connections/Activities

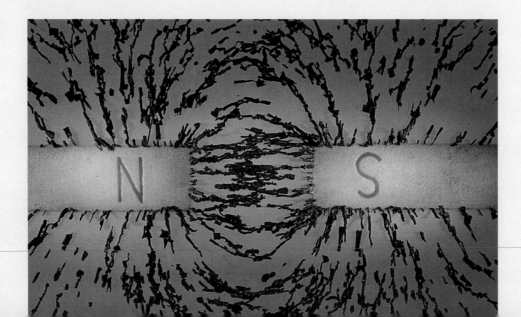

Activities/Science Connections

Science

INTEGRATION

Chemistry: 17
Life Science: 26
Environmental Science: 78

SCIENCE *Online*

Research: 12, 43, 51, 69, 76, 82
Collect Data: 78
Data Update: 25

THE PRINCETON REVIEW

Test Practice: 35, 63, 89, 91, 92–93

Feature Contents

Problem-Solving Activities

Math Skills Activities

Skill Builder Activities

Science

Math

Electricity and Magnetism

Figure 1
Lightning is a discharge of static electricity.

The brilliant flash of lightning during a thunderstorm might not be new to you. But did you know that it is a discharge of static electricity? It took years and the accumulated work of many scientists to form the foundation of modern ideas about magnetism and electricity.

Writings as early as the first century B.C. show that magnetism was a recognized and studied phenomena. Magnetite, a naturally occurring magnetized rock that attracts iron objects, was available and used to study magnetism in ancient civilizations. The origins of practical uses for magnetism, such as in compasses, are unknown but they were used centuries before the first writings about magnetism appeared.

Figure 2
Without electricity cities all over the world, like the one below, would be dark at night.

Research and Development

Petrus Peregrinus de Maricourt, a French scientist, published the first documented research study of magnets in 1269. He used magnetite, or lodestone, and a thin, iron rectangle to study the magnetic field generated by the magnetite. Over 300 years later in 1600, William Gilbert, an English physician, published a book called *Of Magnets, Magnetic Bodies, and the Great Magnet of the Earth*. He studied electricity and magnetism and made the analogy that Earth behaves like a giant magnet.

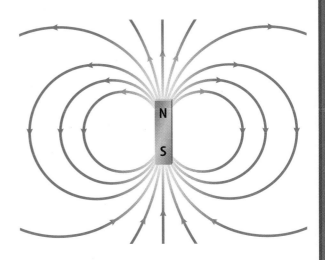

Figure 3
The magnetic field of a bar magnet runs through and around the magnet, from its north pole to its south pole.

The Leyden Jar

In 1746, the Leyden jar was invented by Pieter van Musschenbroek, a Dutch physicist. This provided a cheap and convenient source of electric charges used to study electricity. One form of a Leyden jar is a glass vial partially filled with water that contains a conducting wire capable of storing a large amount of static charge. Benjamin Franklin used a Leyden jar when he flew a silk kite during a thunderstorm to show that lightning was an electrical discharge. Franklin's kite was connected by a key on a wet string attached to a Leyden jar. Without the invention of the Leyden jar, Franklin's experiment would not have been possible.

Magnetism and Electricity are Related

In 1820, Hans Oersted, a Dutch scientist, discovered that current flowing through a wire deflected a compass needle. This discovery showed a link between electricity and magnetism. Later that year, André Ampère, a French scientist, performed extensive studies on the magnetic fields generated by electric currents and established the laws of magnetic force between electric currents. Michael Faraday, an English scientist, heard about Oersted's work and continued to study the relationship between magnetism and electric current. In 1831, he discovered that moving a magnet near a wire induced a current in the wire. Oersted showed that an electric current creates a magnetic field and Faraday showed that a magnetic field creates an electric current.

Figure 4
Iron filings show the shape of magnetic field lines around various magnets.

Maxwell Ties it All Together

James Maxwell, an English physicist, expanded upon Faraday and Oersted's work and translated their experimental findings into mathematics. Maxwell also predicted the existence of electromagnetic waves. He hypothesized that light was an electromagnetic wave. In 1886, Heinrich Hertz, a German physicist, verified the existence of electromagnetic waves when he discovered radio waves.

Electricity and Magnetism Today

These pioneers of science might have had a hard time believing the many ways we use electricity and magnetism today. Our homes contain many devices that use electricity and magnetism. Think about all of the electrical devices that you have used today. Lights, hair dryers, and toasters are just a few of the possibilities that might be on your list. Many of our small appliances contain motors that use both electricity and magnetism to operate. These inventions would not have been possible without the contributions of many scientists.

Physical Science

The study of magnetism and electricity is part of the branch of science known as physical science, or the study of matter and energy. Physical science often is broken into two branches— chemistry and physics. Physics is the study of the interaction between matter and energy. This includes topics such as forces, speed, distance, waves, magnetism, and electricity. Chemistry is the study of the composition, structure, and properties of atoms and matter and the transformations they can undergo.

Figure 5
Huge electric generators like these use the relationship between electricity and magnetism to produce electric current.

The History of Science

The history of magnetism and electricity is an illustration of how science often is the result of the investigations of many people over centuries. Recall that the discovery of the laws that govern magnetism and electricity involved scientists from several countries beginning as early as the first century B.C. This demonstrates the importance of writing and communicating scientific ideas from scientist to scientist and century to century.

Communicating Scientific Ideas

Scientists do not work alone in any field. A good scientist studies historical scientific works as well as contemporary scientific literature. Scientific discoveries must be documented and published so that other scientists can verify results and build upon each other's work. The advancements in electricity and magnetism would have been much slower if each scientist had to rediscover the findings of the scientists before them.

Documenting Scientific Studies

Communication today is almost instantaneous. The telephone, computer, Internet, and fax machine provides us with quick access to people around the world, as well as access to a vast amount of information. There are many ways to document and communicate scientific studies. Journal articles, scientific papers, books, newspaper articles, and web pages are some of the methods that are available today. The documentation of scientific work is as important today as it was centuries ago.

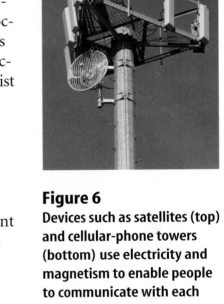

Figure 6
Devices such as satellites (top) and cellular-phone towers (bottom) use electricity and magnetism to enable people to communicate with each other.

A modern traveler might use the Global Positioning System, or GPS, instead of a magnetic compass. GPS is often used for navigation instead of a compass because GPS can pinpoint your location to a high degree of accuracy. Research the development of the GPS system. What types of vehicles use GPS devices? Make a list of some of the ways that GPS is used in agriculture, construction, transportation, and research.

Electricity

This spark generator uses voltages of millions of volts to produce these electric discharges that resemble lightning. Other electric discharges, like those that occur when you walk across a carpeted floor, are not as visible. In your home, electric currents flow through wires, and also power lights, televisions, and other appliances. In this chapter, you will learn about electric charges and the forces they exert on each other. You also will learn how electric charges moving in a circuit can do useful work.

What do you think?

Science Journal Look at the picture below with a classmate. Discuss what this might be. Here's a hint: *Think power—lots of power.* Write your answer or best guess in your Science Journal.

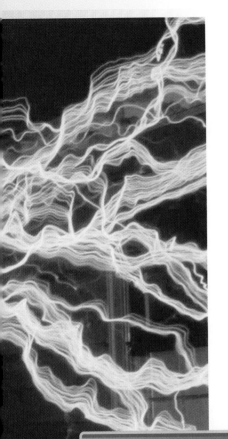

No computers? No CD players? No video games? Can you imagine life without electricity? You depend on it every day, and not just to make life more fun. Electricity heats and cools homes and provides light. It provides energy that can be used to do work. This energy comes from the forces that electric charges exert on each other. What is the nature of these electric forces?

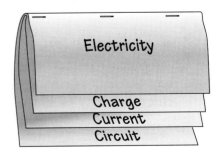

Investigate electric forces

1. Inflate a rubber balloon.
2. Put some small bits of paper on your desktop and bring the balloon close to the bits of paper. Observe what happens.
3. Charge the balloon by holding it by the knot and rubbing the balloon on your hair or on a piece of wool.
4. Bring the balloon close to the bits of paper and observe what happens.
5. Charge two balloons using the procedure in step 3 and bring them close to each other, holding them by their knots.
6. Repeat step 3, then touch the balloon with your hand. Now what happens when you bring the balloon close to the bits of paper?

Observe

Record your observations of electric forces in your Science Journal.

Before You Read

FOLDABLES
Reading & Study
Skills

Making a Vocabulary Study Fold Make the following Foldable to help you better understand the terms *charge, current,* and *circuit.*

1. Stack two sheets of paper in front of you so the short side of both sheets is at the top.
2. Slide the top sheet up so that about 4 cm of the bottom sheet show.
3. Fold both sheets top to bottom to form four tabs and staple along the fold.
4. Label the tabs *Electricity, Charge, Current,* and *Circuit.*
5. Before you read the chapter, write your definition of charge, current, and circuit under the tabs. As you read the chapter, correct your definition and write more information about each.

Electricity

Charge
Current
Circuit

Electric Charge

As You Read

What You'll Learn

- **Describe** how objects can become electrically charged.
- **Explain** how electric charges affect other electric charges.
- **Distinguish** between insulators and conductors.
- **Describe** how electric discharges such as lightning occur.

Vocabulary

ion	insulator
static charge	conductor
electric force	electric discharge
electric field	

Why It's Important

All electrical phenomena result from the behavior of electric charges.

Electricity

You can't see, smell, or taste electricity, so it might seem mysterious. However, electricity is not so hard to understand when you start by thinking small—very small. All solids, liquids, and gases are made of tiny particles called atoms. Atoms, as shown in **Figure 1,** are made of even smaller particles called protons, neutrons, and electrons. Protons and neutrons are held together tightly in the nucleus at the center of an atom, but electrons swarm around the nucleus in all directions. Protons and electrons possess electric charge, but neutrons have no electric charge.

Positive and Negative Charge Two types of electric charge exist—positive and negative. Protons carry a positive charge, and electrons carry a negative charge. The amount of negative charge on an electron is exactly equal to the amount of positive charge on a proton. Because atoms have equal numbers of protons and electrons, the amount of positive charge on all the protons in the nucleus of an atom is exactly balanced by the negative charge on all the electrons moving around the nucleus. Therefore, atoms are electrically neutral, which means they have no overall electric charge.

Some atoms can become negatively charged if they gain extra electrons. Other atoms can easily lose electrons thereby becoming positively charged. A positively or negatively charged atom is called an **ion** (I ahn).

Figure 1
An atom is made of positively charged protons (orange), negatively charged electrons (red), and neutrons (blue) with no electric charge. *Where are the protons and neutrons located in an atom?*

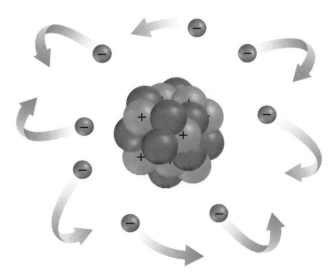

Figure 2
Rubbing can move electrons from one object to another. Because hair holds electrons more loosely than the balloon holds them, electrons are pulled off the hair when the two make contact. *Which object has become positively charged and which has become negatively charged?*

Electrons Move in Solids Electrons can move from atom to atom and from object to object. Rubbing is one way that electrons can be transferred. If you ever have taken clinging clothes from a clothes dryer, you have seen what happens when electrons are transferred from one object to another.

Suppose you rub a balloon on your hair. The atoms in your hair hold their electrons more loosely than the atoms on the balloon hold theirs. As a result, electrons are transferred from the atoms in your hair to the atoms on the surface of the balloon, as shown in **Figure 2.** Because your hair loses electrons, it becomes positively charged. The balloon gains electrons and becomes negatively charged. Your hair and the balloon become attracted to one another and make your hair stand on end. This imbalance of electric charge on an object is called a **static charge.** In solids, static charge is due to the transfer of electrons between objects. Protons cannot be removed easily from the nucleus of an atom and usually do not move from one object to another.

Reading Check *How does an object become electrically charged?*

Ions Move in Solutions Sometimes, a flow of charge can be caused by the movement of ions instead of the movement of electrons. Table salt—sodium chloride—is made of sodium ions and chloride ions that are fixed in place and cannot move through the solid. However, when salt is dissolved in water, the sodium and chloride ions break apart and spread out evenly in the water forming a solution, as shown in **Figure 3.** Now the positive and negative ions are free to move. Solutions containing ions play an important role in enabling different parts of your body to communicate with each other. **Figure 4** shows how a nerve cell uses ions to transmit signals. These signals moving throughout your body enable you to sense, move, and even think.

Figure 3
When table salt (NaCl) dissolves in water, the sodium ions and chloride ions break apart. These ions now are able to carry electric energy.

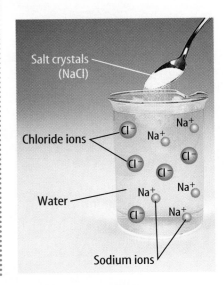

Salt crystals (NaCl)

Chloride ions

Water

Sodium ions

Figure 4

The control and coordination of all your bodily functions involves signals traveling from one part of your body to another through nerve cells. Nerve cells use ions to transmit signals from one nerve cell to another.

A When a nerve cell is not transmitting a signal, it moves positively charged sodium ions (Na$^+$) outside the membrane of the nerve cell. As a result, the outside of the cell membrane becomes positively charged and the inside becomes negatively charged.

C As sodium ions pass through the cell membrane, the inside of the membrane becomes positively charged. This triggers sodium ions next to this area to move back inside the membrane, and an electric impulse begins to move down the nerve cell.

B A chemical released by another nerve cell called a neurotransmitter starts the impulse moving along the cell. At one end of the cell, the neurotransmitter causes sodium ions to move back inside the cell membrane.

D When the impulse reaches the end of the nerve cell, a neurotransmitter is released that causes the next nerve cell to move sodium ions back inside the cell membrane. In this way, the signal is passed from cell to cell.

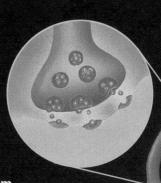

Unlike charges attract.

Like charges repel.   Like charges repel.

Electric Forces

The electrons in an atom swarm around the nucleus. What keeps these electrons close to the nucleus? The positively-charged protons in the nucleus exert an attractive electric force on the negatively-charged electrons. All charged objects exert an **electric force** on each other. The electric force between two charges can be attractive or repulsive, as shown in **Figure 5.** Objects with the same type of charge repel one another and objects with opposite charges attract one another. This rule is often stated as "like charges repel, and unlike charges attract."

The electric force between two electric charges gets stronger as the distance between them decreases. A positive and a negative charge are attracted to each other more strongly if they are closer together. Two like charges are pushed away more strongly from each other the closer they are. The electric force on two objects that are charged, such as two balloons that have been rubbed on wool, also increases if the amount of charge on the objects increases.

Electric Fields You might have noticed examples of how charged objects don't have to be touching to exert an electric force on each other. For instance, two charged balloons push each other apart even though they are not touching. Also, bits of paper and a charged balloon don't have to be touching for the balloon to attract the paper. How are charged objects able to exert forces on each other without toughing?

Electric charges exert a force on each other at a distance through an **electric field** that exists around every electric charge. **Figure 6** shows the electric field around a positive and a negative charge. An electric field gets stronger as you get closer to a charge, just as the electric force between two charges becomes greater as the charges get closer together.

Figure 6
The lines with arrowheads represent the electric field around charges. The direction of each arrow is the direction a positive charge would move if it were placed in the field.

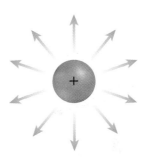

A The electric field arrows point away from a positive charge.

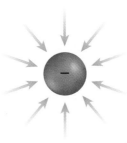

B The electric field arrows point toward a negative charge. *Why are these arrows in the opposite direction of the arrows around the positive charge?*

Figure 7
Electric charges move more easily through conductors than through insulators.

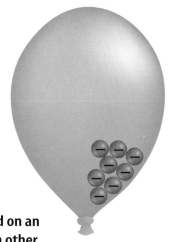

A Charges placed on an insulator repel each other but cannot move easily on the surface of the insulator. As a result, the charges remain in one place.

B Charges placed on a conductor repel each other but can move easily on the conductor's surface. Thus, they spread out as far apart as possible.

Research Visit the Glencoe Science Web site at **science.glencoe.com** for news on recent breakthroughs in superconductor research. Communicate to your class what you learn.

Insulators and Conductors

Rubbing a balloon on your hair transfers electrons from your hair to the balloon. However, only the part of the balloon that was rubbed on your hair becomes charged because electrons cannot move easily through rubber. As a result, the electrons that were rubbed onto the balloon stay in one place, as shown in **Figure 7A.** A material in which electrons cannot move easily from place to place is called an **insulator.** Examples of insulators are plastic, wood, glass, and rubber.

Materials that are **conductors** contain electrons that can move more easily through the material. Look at **Figure 7B.** Excess electrons on the surface of a conductor spread out over the entire surface.

Metals as Conductors The best conductors are metals such as copper, gold, and aluminum. In metal atoms, a few electrons are not attracted as strongly to the nucleus as the other electrons, and are loosely held by the atom. When metal atoms form a solid, the metal atoms can move only short distances. However, the electrons that are loosely-held by the atoms can move easily through the solid piece of metal. In an insulator, the electrons are held tightly in the atoms that make up the insulator and therefore cannot move easily.

An electric wire is made from a conductor coated with an insulator such as plastic. Electrons move easily through the copper but do not move easily through the plastic insulation. This prevents electrons from moving through the insulation and causing an electric shock if someone touches the wire.

Induced Charge

Has this ever happened to you? You walk across a carpet and as you reach for a metal doorknob, you feel an electric shock. Maybe you even see a spark jump between your fingertip and the doorknob. To find out what happened, look at **Figure 8.**

As you walk, electrons are rubbed off the rug by your shoes. The electrons then spread over the surface of your skin. As you bring your hand close to the doorknob, the electric field around the excess electrons on your hand repel the electrons in the doorknob. Because the doorknob is a good conductor, its electrons move easily. The part of the doorknob closest to your hand then becomes positively charged. This separation of positive and negative charges due to an electric field is called an induced charge.

If the electric field in the space between your hand and the knob is strong enough, charge can be pulled across that space, as shown in **Figure 8C.** This rapid movement of excess charge from one place to another is an **electric discharge.** Lightning is also an electric discharge. In a storm cloud, air currents cause the bottom of the cloud to become negatively charged. This negative charge induces a positive charge in the ground below the cloud. Lightning occurs when electric charge moves between the cloud and the ground.

Lightning can occur in ways other than from a cloud to the ground. To find out more about lightning, see the **Lightning Field Guide** at the back of the book.

Figure 8
A spark that jumps between your fingers and a metal doorknob starts at your feet.

A As you walk across the floor, you rub electrons from the carpet onto the bottom of your shoes. These electrons then spread out over your skin, including your hands.

B As you bring your hand close to the metal doorknob, electrons on the doorknob move as far away from your hand as possible. The part of the doorknob closest to your hand is left with a positive charge.

C The attractive electric force between the electrons on your hand and the induced positive charge on the doorknob might be strong enough to pull electrons from your hand to the doorknob. You might see this as a spark and feel a mild electric shock.

Grounding

Lightning is an electric discharge that can cause damage and injury because a lightning bolt releases an extremely large amount of electric energy. Even electric discharges that release small amounts of energy can damage delicate circuitry in devices such as computers. One way to avoid the damage caused by electric discharges is to make the excess charges flow harmlessly into Earth's surface. Earth can be a conductor, and because it is so large, it can absorb an enormous quantity of excess charge.

The process of providing a pathway to drain excess charge into Earth is called grounding. The pathway is usually a conductor such as a wire or a pipe. You might have noticed lightning rods at the top of buildings and towers, as shown in **Figure 9.** These rods are made of metal and are connected to metal cables that conduct electric charge into the ground if the rod is struck by lightning.

Figure 9
A lightning rod can protect a building from being damaged by a lightning strike. *Should a lightning rod be an insulator or a conductor?*

 Reading Check *How can tall structures be protected against lightning strikes?*

Section 1 Assessment

1. What is the difference between an object that is negatively charged and one that is positively charged?

2. Two electrically charged objects repel each other. What can you say about the type of charge on each object?

3. Contrast insulators and conductors. List three materials that are good insulators and three that are good conductors.

4. Why does an electric discharge occur?

5. **Think Critically** Excess charge placed on the surface of a conductor tends to spread over the entire surface, but excess charge placed on an insulator tends to stay where it was placed originally. Explain.

Skill Builder Activities

6. **Recognizing Cause and Effect** Clothes that are dried on a clothesline outdoors don't stick to each other when they are taken out of the laundry basket. Clothes that are dried in a clothes dryer do tend to stick to each other. What is the reason for this difference? **For more help, refer to the** Science Skill Handbook.

7. **Communicating** You are sitting in a car. You slide out of the car seat, and as you start to touch the metal car door, a spark jumps from your hand to the door. In your Science Journal, describe how the spark was formed. Use at least four vocabulary words in your explanation. **For more help, refer to the** Science Skill Handbook.

Electric Current

Flow of Charge

An electric discharge, such as a lightning bolt, can release a huge amount of energy in an instant. However, electric lights, refrigerators, TVs, and stereos need a steady source of electric energy that can be controlled. This source of electric energy comes from an **electric current,** which is the flow of electric charge. In solids, the flowing charges are electrons. In liquids, the flowing charges are ions, which can be positively or negatively charged. Electric current is measured in units of amperes (A). A model for electric current is flowing water. Water flows downhill because a gravitational force acts on it. Similarly, electrons flow because an electric force acts on them.

A Model for a Simple Circuit How does a flow of water provide energy? If the water is separated from Earth by using a pump, the higher water now has gravitational potential energy, as shown in **Figure 10.** As the water falls and does work on the waterwheel, the water loses potential energy and the waterwheel gains kinetic energy. For the water to flow continuously, it must flow through a closed loop. Electric charges will flow continuously only through a closed conducting loop called a **circuit.**

As You Read

What You'll Learn

- **Relate** voltage to the electric energy carried by an electric current.
- **Describe** a battery and how it produces an electric current.
- **Explain** electrical resistance.

Vocabulary

electric current   voltage
circuit   resistance

Why It's Important

The electric appliances you use rely on electric current.

Figure 10

The potential energy of water is increased when a pump raises the water above Earth. The greater the height is, the more energy the water has. *How can this energy be used?*

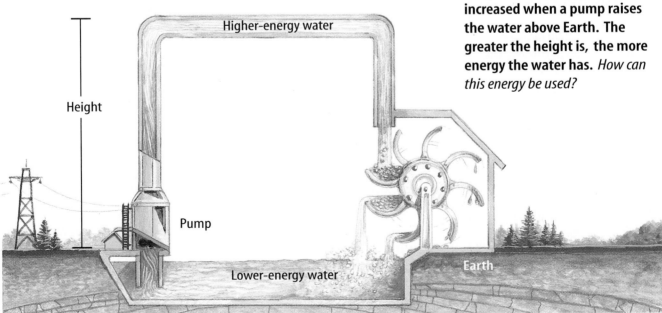

Figure 11

As long as there is a closed path for electrons to follow, electrons flow in a circuit from the negative battery terminal to the positive terminal.

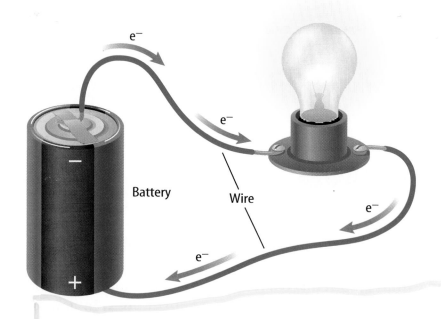

Electric Circuits The simplest electric circuit contains a source of electrical energy, such as a battery, and an electric conductor, such as a wire, connected to the battery. For the simple circuit shown in **Figure 11,** a closed path is formed by wires connected to a lightbulb and to a battery. Electric current flows in the circuit as long as none of the wires, including the glowing filament wire in the lightbulb, is disconnected or broken.

Voltage In a water circuit, a pump increases the gravitational potential energy of the water by raising the water from a lower level to a higher level. In an electric circuit, a battery increases the electric potential energy of electrons. This electric potential energy can be transformed into other forms of energy. The voltage of a battery is a measure of how much electric potential energy each electron can gain. As voltage increases, more electric potential energy is available to be transformed into other forms of energy. Voltage is measured in volts (V).

How a Current Flows You may think that when an electric current flows in a circuit, electrons travel completely around the circuit. Actually, individual electrons move slowly through a wire in an electric circuit. When the ends of the wire are connected to a battery, electrons in the wire begin to move toward the positive battery terminal. As an electron moves it collides with other electric charges in the wire, and is deflected in a different direction. After each collision, the electron again starts moving toward the positive terminal. A single electron may undergo more than ten trillion collisions each second. As a result, it may take several minutes for an electron in the wire to travel one centimeter.

TRY AT HOME

Mini LAB

Investigating the Electric Force

Procedure
1. Pour a layer of **salt** on a **plate.**
2. Sparingly sprinkle grains of **pepper** on top of the salt. Do not use too much pepper.
3. Rub a **rubber** or **plastic comb** on an article of **wool clothing.**
4. Slowly drag the comb through the salt and observe.

Analysis
1. How did the salt and pepper react to the comb?
2. Explain why the pepper reacted differently than the salt.

Batteries A battery supplies energy to an electric circuit. When the positive and negative terminals in a battery are connected in a circuit, the electric potential energy of the electrons in the circuit is increased. As these electrons move toward the positive battery terminal, this electric potential energy is transformed into other forms of energy, just as gravitational potential energy is converted into kinetic energy as water falls.

A battery supplies energy to an electric circuit by converting chemical energy to electric potential energy. For the alkaline battery shown in **Figure 12,** the two terminals are separated by a moist paste. Chemical reactions in the moist paste cause electrons to be transferred to the negative terminal from the atoms in the positive terminal. As a result, the negative terminal becomes negatively charged and the positive terminal becomes positively charged. This causes electrons in the circuit to be pushed away from the negative terminal and to be attracted to the positive terminal.

Battery Life Batteries don't supply energy forever. Maybe you know someone whose car wouldn't start after the lights had been left on overnight? Why do batteries run down? Batteries contain only a limited amount of the chemicals that react to produce chemical energy. These reactions go on as the battery is used and the chemicals are changed into other compounds. Once the original chemicals are used up, the chemical reactions stop and the battery is "dead."

Chemistry
INTEGRATION

Many chemicals are used to make an alkaline battery. Zinc is a source of electrons and positive ions, manganese dioxide is used to collect the electrons at the positive terminal, and water is used to carry ions through the battery. Visit the Glencoe Science Web site at **science.glencoe.com** for information about the chemistry of batteries.

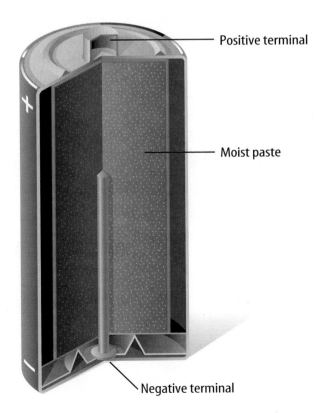

Positive terminal

Moist paste

Negative terminal

Figure 12
When this alkaline battery is connected in an electric circuit, chemical reactions occur in the moist paste of this alkaline battery that move electrons from the positive terminal to the negative terminal.

Resistance

Electrons can move much more easily through conductors than through insulators, but even conductors interfere somewhat with the flow of electrons. The measure of how difficult it is for electrons to flow through a material is called **resistance.** The unit of resistance is the ohm (Ω). Insulators generally have much higher resistance than conductors.

As electrons flow through a circuit, they collide with the atoms and other electric charges in the materials that make up the circuit. Look at **Figure 13.** These collisions cause some of the electrons' electric energy to be converted into thermal energy—heat—and sometimes into light. The amount of electric energy that is converted into heat and light depends on the resistance of the materials in the circuit.

Wires and Filaments The amount of electric energy that is converted into thermal energy increases as the resistance of the wire increases. Copper, which is one of the best electric conductors, has low resistance. Copper is used in household wiring because little electric energy is lost as electrons flow through copper wires. As a result, not much heat is produced. Because copper wires don't heat up much, the wires don't become hot enough to melt through their insulation, which makes fires less likely to occur. On the other hand, tungsten wire has a higher resistance. As electrons flow through tungsten wire, it becomes extremely hot—so hot, in fact, that it glows with a bright light. The high temperature makes tungsten a poor choice for household wiring, but the light it gives off makes it an excellent choice for the filaments of lightbulbs.

✔ **Reading Check** *Is having resistance in electrical wires ever beneficial?*

Figure 13
As electrons flow through a wire, they travel in a zigzag path as they collide with atoms and other electrons. These collisions cause the electrons to lose some electric energy. *Where does this electric energy go?*

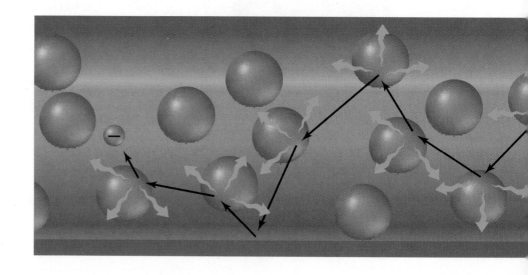

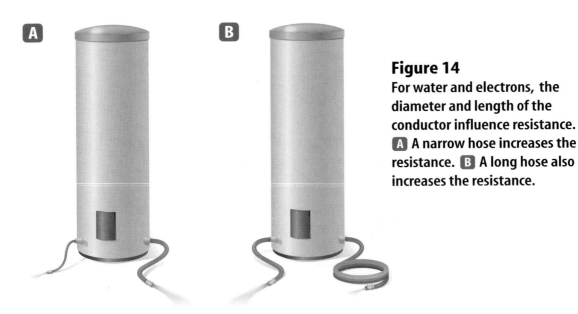

Figure 14
For water and electrons, the diameter and length of the conductor influence resistance. **A** A narrow hose increases the resistance. **B** A long hose also increases the resistance.

Slowing the Flow The electric resistance of a wire also depends on the length and thickness of the wire. Imagine water flowing through a hose, as shown in **Figure 14.** As the hose becomes more narrow or longer, the water flow decreases. In a similar way, the length and diameter of a wire affects electron flow. The electric resistance increases as the wire becomes longer or as it becomes narrower.

Section Assessment

1. How does increasing the voltage in a circuit affect the energy of the electrons flowing in the circuit?

2. How does a battery cause electrons to move in an electric circuit?

3. For the same length, which has more resistance—a garden hose or a fire hose? Which has more resistance—a thin wire or a thick wire?

4. Why is copper often used in household wiring?

5. **Think Critically** Some electrical devices require two batteries, usually placed end to end. How does the voltage of the combination compare with the voltage of a single battery? Try it.

Skill Builder Activities

6. **Drawing Conclusions** Observe the size of various batteries, such as a watch battery, a camera battery, a flashlight battery, and an automobile battery. Conclude whether the voltage produced by a battery is related to its physical size. **For more help, refer to the** Science Skill Handbook.

7. **Communicating** The terms *circuit, current,* and *resistance* are often used in everyday language. In your Science Journal, record several different ways of using the words *circuit, current,* and *resistance.* Compare and contrast the everyday use of the words with their scientific definitions. **For more help, refer to the** Science Skill Handbook.

Electric Circuits

As You Read

What You'll Learn

- **Explain** how voltage, current, and resistance are related in an electric circuit.
- **Investigate** the difference between series and parallel circuits.
- **Determine** the electric power used in a circuit.
- **Describe** how to avoid dangerous electric shock.

Vocabulary

Ohm's law   parallel circuit
series circuit   electric power

Why It's Important

Electric circuits enable the flow of electric current to be controlled in all electrical devices.

Controlling the Current

When you connect a conductor, such as a wire or a lightbulb, between the positive and negative terminals of a battery, electrons flow in the circuit. The amount of current is determined by the voltage supplied by the battery and the resistance of the conductor. To help understand this relationship, imagine a bucket with a hose at the bottom, as shown in **Figure 15.** If the bucket is raised, water will flow out of the hose faster than before. Increasing the height will increase the current.

Voltage and Resistance Think back to the pump and waterwheel in **Figure 10.** Recall that the raised water has energy that is lost when the water falls. Increasing the height from which the water falls increases the energy of the water. Increasing the height of the water is similar to increasing the voltage of the battery. Just as the water current increases when the height of the water increases, the electric current in a circuit increases as voltage increases.

If the diameter of the tube in **Figure 15** is decreased, resistance is greater and the flow of the water decreases. In the same way, as the resistance in an electric circuit increases, the current in the circuit decreases.

Figure 15
Raising the bucket higher increases the potential energy of the water in the bucket. This causes the water to flow out of the hose faster.

Ohm's Law A nineteenth-century German physicist, Georg Simon Ohm, carried out experiments that measured how changing the voltage and resistance in a circuit affected the current. The relationship he found among voltage, current and resistance is now known as **Ohm's law.** In equation form, Ohm's law is written as follows.

$$\text{current} = \frac{\text{voltage}}{\text{resistance}}$$

$$I\,(\text{A}) = \frac{V\,(\text{V})}{R\,(\Omega)}$$

According to Ohm's law, when the voltage in a circuit increases the current increases, just as water flows faster from a bucket that is raised higher. However, when the resistance is increased, the current in the circuit decreases.

Math Skills Activity

Calculating the Current in a Lightbulb

Example Problem

In homes, the standard electric outlet provides 110 V. What is the current through a lightbulb with a resistance of 220 Ω?

Solution

1 *This is what you know:*   voltage: $V = 110$ V
                                                   resistance: $R = 220\ \Omega$

2 *This is what you need to find:*   current: I

3 *This is the equation you need to use:* $I = V/R$

4 *Substitute the known values:* $I = (110\text{ V})/(220\ \Omega)$
                                                     $= 0.5$ A

Check your answer by multiplying it by the resistance of 220 Ω. Do you calculate the given voltage of 110 V?

Practice Problems

1. What is the resistance of a lightbulb connected to a 110-V outlet that requires a current of 0.2 A?
2. Which draws more current at the same voltage, a lightbulb with higher resistance or a lightbulb with lower resistance? Use a mathematical example to answer this question.

For more help, refer to the Math Skill Handbook.

Mini LAB

Identifying Simple Circuits

Procedure

1. The filament in a lightbulb is a piece of wire. For the bulb to light, an electric current must flow through the filament in a complete circuit. Examine the base of a **flashlight bulb** carefully. Where are the ends of the filament connected to the base?

2. Connect one piece of **wire,** a **battery,** and a flashlight bulb to make the bulb light. (There are four possible ways to do this.)

Analysis

Draw and label a diagram showing the path that is followed by the electrons in your circuit. Explain your diagram.

Series and Parallel Circuits

Circuits control the movement of electric current by providing paths for electrons to follow. For current to flow, the circuit must provide an unbroken path for current to follow. Have you ever been putting up holiday lights and had a string that would not light because a single bulb was missing or had burned out and you couldn't figure out which one it was? Maybe you've noticed that some strings of lights don't go out no matter how many bulbs burn out or are removed. These two strings of holiday lights are examples of the two kinds of basic circuits—series and parallel.

Wired in a Line   A **series circuit** is a circuit that has only one path for the electric current to follow, as shown in **Figure 16.** If this path is broken, then the current no longer will flow and all the devices in the circuit stop working. If the entire string of lights went out when only one bulb burned out, then the lights in the string were wired as a series circuit. When the bulb burned out, the filament in the bulb broke and the current path through the entire string was broken.

✔ **Reading Check**   *How many different paths can electric current follow in a series circuit?*

In a series circuit, electrical devices are connected along the same current path. As a result, the current is the same through every device. However, each new device that is added to the circuit decreases the current throughout the circuit. This is because each device has electrical resistance, and in a series circuit, the total resistance to the flow of electrons increases as each additional device is added to the circuit. By Ohm's law, as the resistance increases, the current decreases.

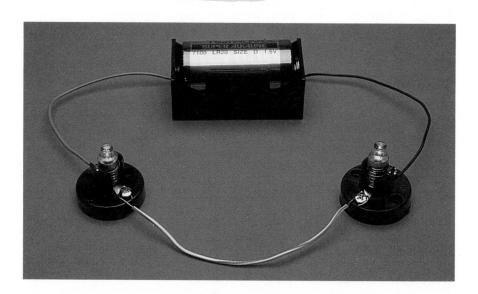

Figure 16
This circuit is an example of a series circuit. A series circuit has only one path for electric current to follow. *What happens to the current in this circuit if any of the connecting wires are removed?*

Branched Wiring What if you wanted to watch TV and had to turn on all the lights, a hair dryer, and every other electrical appliance in the house to do so? That's what it would be like if all the electrical appliances in your house were connected in a series circuit.

Instead, houses, schools, and other buildings are wired using parallel circuits. A **parallel circuit** is a circuit that has more than one path for the electric current to follow, as shown in **Figure 17.** The current branches so that electrons flow through each of the paths. If one path is broken, electrons continue to flow through the other paths. Adding or removing additional devices in one branch does not break the current path in the other branches, so the devices on those branches continue to work normally.

In a parallel circuit, the resistance in each branch can be different, depending on the devices in the branch. The lower the resistance is in a branch, the more current flows in the branch. So the current in each branch of a parallel circuit can be different.

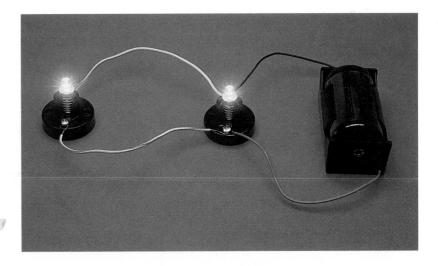

Figure 17
This circuit is an example of a parallel circuit. A parallel circuit has more than one path for electric current to follow. *What happens to the current in the circuit if either of the wires connecting the two lightbulbs is removed?*

Protecting Electric Circuits

In a parallel circuit, the current that flows out of the battery or electric outlet increases as more devices are added to the circuit. As the current through the circuit increases, the wires heat up.

To keep the wire from becoming hot enough to cause a fire, the circuits in houses and other buildings have fuses or circuit breakers like those shown in **Figure 18** that limit the amount of current in the wiring. When the current becomes larger than 15 A or 20 A, a piece of metal in the fuse melts or a switch in the circuit breaker opens, stopping the current. The cause of the overload can then be removed, and the circuit can be used again by replacing the fuse or resetting the circuit breaker.

A In some buildings, each circuit is connected to a fuse. The fuses are usually located in a fuse box.

Figure 18
You might have fuses in your home that prevent electric wires from overheating.

Wire

B A fuse contains a piece of wire that melts and breaks when the current flowing through the fuse becomes too large.

Table 1 Power Ratings of Common Appliances

Appliance	Power (W)
Computer	150
Color TV	140
Stereo	60
Refrigerator	350
Toaster	1,100
Microwave	800
Hair dryer	1,200

Electric Power

Electric energy is used in many ways to do useful jobs. Toasters and electric ovens convert electric energy to heat, stereos convert electric energy to sound, and a fan blade rotates as electric energy is converted to mechanical energy. The rate at which an appliance converts electric energy to another form of energy is the **electric power** used by the appliance.

Calculating Power The rate at which energy is used in the circuit is related to the amount of energy carried by the electrons, which increases as the voltage increases. The power that is used also is related to the rate at which electrons flow into the circuit. As a result, the power that is used in a circuit can be determined by multiplying the current by the voltage.

$$\text{Power} = \text{current} \times \text{voltage}$$
$$P\,(\text{W}) = I\,(\text{A}) \times V\,(\text{V})$$

Table 1 lists the power required by several common appliances. The unit of power is the watt, W.

Math Skills Activity

Calculating the Electric Power Used by a Lightbulb

Example Problem

How much power does a lightbulb use if the current is 0.55 A and the voltage is 110 V?

Solution

1 *This is what you know:* voltage: $V = 110$ V
current: $I = 0.55$ A

2 *This is what you need to find:* power: P

3 *This is the equation you need to use:* $P = I \times V$

4 *Substitute the known values:* $P = 0.55$ A $\times$ 110 V
$= 60$ W

Check your answer by dividing it by the current of 0.55 A. Did you calculate the given voltage of 110 V?

> **Practice Problem**
>
> How much current does a 25-W bulb require in a 110-V circuit?

For more help, refer to the Math Skill Handbook.

Cost of Electric Energy Power is the rate at which energy is used, or the amount of energy that is used per second. When you use a hair dryer, the amount of electric energy that is used depends on the power of the hair dryer and the amount of time you use it. If you used it for 5 min yesterday and 10 min today, you used twice as much energy today as yesterday.

Using electric energy costs money. Electric companies generate electric energy and sell it in units of kilowatt-hours to homes, schools, and businesses. One kilowatt-hour, kWh, is an amount of electric energy equal to using 1 kW of power continuously for 1 h. This would be the amount of energy needed to light ten 100-W lightbulbs for 1 h, or one 100-W lightbulb for 10 h.

 **Reading Check** *What does kWh stand for and what does it measure?*

An electric company usually charges its customers for the number of kilowatt-hours they use every month. The number of kilowatt-hours used in a building such as a house or a school is measured by an electric meter, which usually is attached to the outside of the building, as shown in **Figure 19.**

Figure 19
Electric meters measure the amount of electric energy used in kilowatt-hours. *Find the electric meter that records the electric energy used in your house.*

Electrical Safety

 **Health**
INTEGRATION

Have you ever had a mild electric shock? You probably felt only a mild tingling sensation, but electricity can have much more dangerous effects. In 1997, electric shocks killed an estimated 490 people in the United States. **Table 2** lists a few safety tips to help prevent electrical accidents.

Data Update Visit the Glencoe Science Web site at **science.glencoe.com** to find the cost of electric energy in various parts of the world. Communicate to your class what you learn.

Table 2 Situations to Avoid

Never use appliances with frayed or damaged electric cords.
Unplug appliances before working on them, such as when prying toast out of a jammed toaster.
Avoid all water when using plugged-in appliances.
Never touch power lines with anything, including kite string and ladders.
Always respect warning signs and labels.

The scale below shows how the effect of electric current on the human body depends on the amount of current that flows into the body.

0.0005 A	Tingle
0.001 A	Pain threshold
0.01 A	Inability to let go
0.025 A	
0.05 A	Difficulty breathing
0.10 A	
0.25 A	
0.50 A	Heart failure
1.00 A	

Electric Shock You experience an electric shock when an electric current enters your body. In some ways your body is like a piece of insulated wire. The fluids inside your body are good conductors of current. The electrical resistance of dry skin is much higher. Skin insulates the body like the plastic insulation around a copper wire. Your skin helps keep electric current from entering your body.

A current can enter your body when you accidentally become part of an electric circuit. Whether you receive a deadly shock depends on the amount of current that flows into your body. The current that flows through the wires connected to a 60 W light-bulb is 0.5 A. This amount of current entering your body could be deadly. Even a current as small as 0.001 A can be painful.

Lightning Safety On average, more people are killed every year by lightning in the United States than by hurricanes or tornadoes. Most lightning deaths and injuries occur outdoors. If you are outside and can see lightning or hear thunder, you should take shelter in a large, enclosed building if possible. A metal vehicle such as a car, bus, or van can provide protection if you avoid contact with metal surfaces.

You should avoid high places and open fields, and stay away from isolated high objects such as trees, flagpoles, or light towers. Avoid picnic shelters, baseball dugouts, bleachers, metal fences, and bodies of water. If you are caught outdoors, get in the lightning-safety position—squat low to the ground on the balls of your feet with your hands on your knees.

Section Assessment

1. As the resistance in a simple circuit increases, what happens to the current?

2. What are the differences between a series circuit and a parallel circuit?

3. You have the stereo on while you're working on the computer. Which appliance is using more power?

4. How is your body like a piece of insulated wire?

5. **Think Critically** What determines whether a 100-W lightbulb costs more to use than a 1,200-W hair dryer does?

Skill Builder Activities

6. **Making and Using Tables** Suppose using 1,000 W for 1 h costs $0.08. Calculate the cost of using each of the appliances in **Table 1** for 24 h. Present your results in a table. **For more help, refer to the** Science Skill Handbook.

7. **Using Proportions** A typical household uses 1,000 kWh of electrical energy every month. If a power company supplies electrical energy to 10,000 households, how much electrical energy must it supply every year? **For more help, refer to the** Math Skill Handbook.

Activity

Current in a Parallel Circuit

In this activity, you will investigate how the current in a circuit changes when two or more lightbulbs are connected in parallel. Because the brightness of a lightbulb increases or decreases as more or less current flows through it, the brightness of the bulbs in the circuits can be used to determine which circuit has more current.

Materials

1.5-V lightbulbs (4)
1.5-V batteries (2)
10-cm-long pieces of insulated wire (8)

battery holders (2)
minibulb sockets (4)

What You'll Investigate

How does connecting devices in parallel affect the electric current in a circuit?

Goal

■ **Observe** how the current in a parallel circuit changes as more devices are added.

Safety Precautions

Procedure

1. Connect one lightbulb to the battery in a complete circuit. After you've made the bulb light, disconnect the bulb from the battery to keep the battery from running down. This circuit will be the brightness tester.

2. Make a parallel circuit by connecting two bulbs as shown in the diagram. Reconnect the bulb in the brightness tester and compare its brightness with the brightness of the two bulbs in the parallel circuit. Record your observations.

3. Add another bulb to the parallel circuit as shown in the figure. How does the brightness of the bulbs change?

4. Disconnect one bulb in the parallel circuit. What happens to the brightness of the remaining bulbs?

Conclude and Apply

1. Compared to the brightness tester, is the current in the parallel circuit more or less?
2. How does adding additional devices affect the current in a parallel circuit?
3. Are the electric circuits in your house wired in series or parallel? How do you know?

Communicating Your Data

Compare your conclusions with those of other students in your class. **For more help, refer to the** Science Skill Handbook.

Activity

A Model for Voltage and Current

The flow of electrons in an electric circuit is something like the flow of water in a hose connected to a water tank. By raising or lowering the height of the tank, you can increase or decrease the potential energy of the water. In this activity you will model the flow of current in a circuit by investigating how the flow of water in a tube depends on the diameter of the tube and the height the water falls.

What You'll Investigate

How is the flow of water through a tube affected by changing the height of a container of water and the diameter of the tube?

Materials

plastic funnel
rubber or plastic tubing of different
    diameters (1 m each)
meterstick
ring stand with ring
stopwatch
*clock displaying seconds
hose clamp
*binder clip
500-mL beakers (2)
*Alternate Materials

Goal

■ **Model** the flow of current in a simple circuit.

Safety Precautions 👓 🧤

Flow Rate Data

Trial	Height (cm)	Diameter (mm)	Time (s)	Flow Rate (mL/s)
1				
2				
3				
4				

Procedure

1. **Design** a data table in which to record your data. It should be similar to the table on the previous page.

2. Connect the tubing to the bottom of the funnel and place the funnel in the ring of the ring stand.

3. **Measure** the inside diameter of the rubber tubing. Record your data.

4. Place a 500-mL beaker at the bottom of the ring stand and lower the ring so the open end of the tubing is in the beaker.

5. Use the meterstick to measure the height from the top of the funnel to the bottom of the ring stand.

6. Working with a classmate, pour water into the funnel fast enough to keep the funnel full but not overflowing. Measure and record the time needed for 100 mL of water to flow into the beaker. Use the hose clamp to start and stop the flow of water.

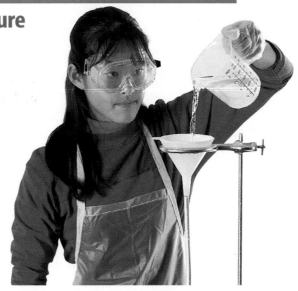

7. Connect tubing with a different diameter to the funnel and repeat steps 2 through 6.

8. Reconnect the original piece of tubing and repeat steps 4 through 6 for several lower positions of the funnel, lowering the height by 10 cm each time.

9. **Calculate** the rate of flow for each trial by dividing 100 mL by the measured time.

Conclude and Apply

1. Make a graph that shows how the rate of flow depends on the funnel height. How does the rate of flow depend on the height of the funnel?

2. How does the rate of flow depend on the diameter of the tubing? Is this what you expected to happen? Explain.

3. Which of the variables that you changed in your trials corresponds to the voltage in a circuit? The resistance?

4. Based on your results, how would the current in a circuit depend on the voltage? How would the current depend on the resistance?

*C*ommunicating
Your Data

Share your graph with other students in your class. Did other students draw the same conclusions as you? **For more help, refer to the** Science Skill Handbook.

Fire in the Forest

Smokey the Bear is partly correct—most forest fires are started by people either deliberately or accidentally. However, some fires are caused by nature. Though lightning is responsible for only about ten percent of forest fires, it causes about one half of all fire damage. For example, in 2000, fires set by lightning raged in 12 states at the same time, burning nearly 20,000 km^2 of land. That is roughly equal in area to the state of Massachusetts. Fires sparked by lightning often strike in remote, difficult-to-reach areas, such as national parks and range lands.

Burning undetected for days, these fires can spread out of control and are hard to extinguish. Sometimes, firefighters must jump into the heart of these blazing areas to put the fires out. In addition to threatening lives, the fires can destroy millions of dollars worth of homes and property. Air pollution caused by smoke from forest fires also can have harmful effects on people. When wood products and fossil fuels are burned, they release particulate matter into the atmosphere. This can damage the human respiratory system, especially for those with preexisting conditions, such as asthma.

People aren't the only victims of forest fires. The fires kill animals, as well. Those who survive the blaze often perish because their habitats have been destroyed. Monster blazes also cause damage to the environment. They spew carbon dioxide and other gases into the atmosphere. Some of these gases may contribute to the greenhouse effect that warms the planet. In addition, fires give off carbon monoxide, which can cause ozone to form. In the lower atmosphere, ozone can damage vegetation, kill trees, and irritate lung tissue. Moreover, massive forest fires harm the logging industry, cause soil erosion in the ruined land, and are responsible for the loss of water reserves that normally collect in a healthy forest.

Plant life returns after a forest fire in Yellowstone National Park.

But fires caused by lightning also have some positive effects. In old, thick forests, trees often become diseased and insect-ridden. By removing these unhealthy trees, fires allow healthy trees greater access to water and nutrients. Fires also clean away a forest's dead trees, underbrush, and needles. This not only clears out space for new vegetation, it provides new food for them, as well. Dead organic matter returns its nutrients to the ground as it decays, but it can take a century for dead logs to rot completely.

Fires ignited by lightning might not be all bad

A fire completes the decay process almost instantly, allowing nutrients to be recycled a lot faster. The removal of these combustible materials prevents more widespread fires from occurring. It also lets new grasses and trees grow on the burned ground. The new types of vegetation attract new types of animals. This, in turn, creates a healthier and more diverse forest.

CONNECTIONS Research Find out more about the job of putting out forest fires. What training is needed? What gear do firefighters wear? Why would people risk their lives to save a forest? Use the media center to learn more about forest firefighters and their careers. Report to the class.

Chapter **1** Study Guide

Reviewing Main Ideas

Section 1 Electric Charge

1. The two types of electric charge are positive and negative. Like charges repel and unlike charges attract.

2. An object becomes negatively charged if it gains electrons and positively charged if it loses electrons.

3. Electrically charged objects have an electric field surrounding them and exert electric forces on one another.

4. Electrons can move easily in conductors, but not so easily in insulators. *Why isn't the building shown below harmed when lightning strikes it?*

Section 2 Electric Current

1. Electric current is the flow of charges—usually either electrons or ions.

2. The energy carried by the current in a circuit increases as the voltage in the circuit increases.

3. In a battery chemical reactions provide the energy that causes electrons to flow in a circuit.

4. As electrons flow in a circuit, some of their electrical energy is lost due to resistance in the circuit. *In a simple circuit, why do electrons stop flowing if the circuit is broken?*

Section 3 Electric Circuits

1. In an electric circuit, the voltage, current, and resistance are related by Ohm's law, expressed as $I = V/R$.

2. The two basic kinds of electric circuits are parallel circuits and series circuits. A series circuit has only one path for the current to follow, but a parallel circuit has more than one path.

3. The rate at which electric devices use electrical energy is the electric power used by the device. Electric companies charge customers for using electrical energy in units of kilowatt-hours.

4. The amount of current flowing through the body determines how much damage occurs. The current from wall outlets can be dangerous. *Hair dryers often come with a reset button. What is the purpose of the button, and how might the reset mechanism work?*

FOLDABLES
Reading & Study Skills

After You Read

Using the information on your Foldable, under the *Electricity* tab, explain the differences between the two types of charges and between the two types of circuits.

Visualizing Main Ideas

Correctly order the following concept map, which illustrates how electric current moves through a simple circuit.

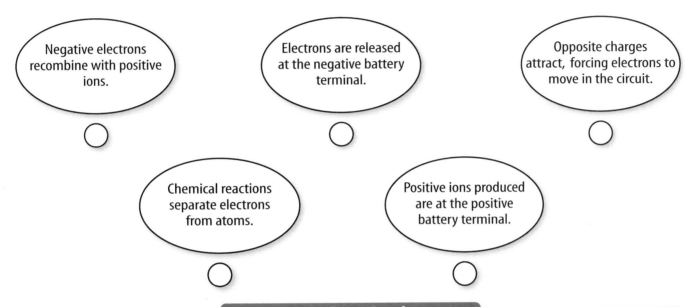

Negative electrons recombine with positive ions.

Electrons are released at the negative battery terminal.

Opposite charges attract, forcing electrons to move in the circuit.

Chemical reactions separate electrons from atoms.

Positive ions produced are at the positive battery terminal.

Vocabulary Review

Vocabulary Words

a. circuit
b. conductor
c. electric current
d. electric discharge
e. electric field
f. electric force
g. electric power
h. insulator
i. ion
j. Ohm's law
k. parallel circuit
l. resistance
m. series circuit
n. static charge
o. voltage

Study Tip

Whether or not you've taken a particular type of test or practiced for an exam many times, it's a good idea to start by reading the instructions provided at the beginning of each section. It only takes a moment.

Using Vocabulary

Answer the following questions using complete sentences.

1. What is the term for the flow of charge?

2. What is the relationship among voltage, current, and resistance in a circuit?

3. In which material do electrons move easily?

4. What is the name for the unbroken path that current follows?

5. What is the term for an excess of electric charge in one place?

6. What is an atom that has lost or gained electrons called?

7. Which circuits have more than one path for electrons to follow?

8. What is the rate at which electrical energy is converted to other forms of energy?

Checking Concepts

Choose the word or phrase that best answers the question.

1. An object that is positively charged _____ .
   A) has more neutrons than protons
   B) has more protons than electrons
   C) has more electrons than protons
   D) has more electrons than neutrons

2. What is the force between two electrons?
   A) unbalanced   C) attractive
   B) neutral   D) repulsive

3. How much power does the average hair dryer use?
   A) 20 W   C) 750 W
   B) 75 W   D) 1,200 W

4. What property of a wire increases when it is made thinner?
   A) resistance   C) current
   B) voltage   D) charge

5. What property does Earth have that causes grounding to drain static charges?
   A) It is a planet.
   B) It has a high resistance.
   C) It is a conductor.
   D) It is like a battery.

6. Why is a severe electric shock dangerous?
   A) It can stop the heart from beating.
   B) It can cause burns.
   C) It can interfere with breathing.
   D) All of the above are true.

7. Because an air conditioner uses more electric power than a lightbulb in a given amount of time, what also must be true?
   A) It must have a higher resistance.
   B) It must use more energy every second.
   C) It must have its own batteries.
   D) It must be wired in series.

8. What unit of electrical energy is sold by electric companies?
   A) ampere   C) volt
   B) ohm   D) kilowatt-hour

9. What surrounds electric charges that causes them to affect each other even though they are not touching?
   A) an induced charge   C) a conductor
   B) a static discharge   D) an electric field

10. As more devices are added to a series circuit, what happens to the current?
    A) decreases   C) stays the same
    B) increases   D) stops

Thinking Critically

11. Why do materials have electrical resistance?

12. Explain why a balloon that has a static charge will stick to a wall.

13. If you connect two batteries in parallel, will the lightbulb glow brighter than if just one battery is used? Explain, using water as an analogy.

14. If you have two charged objects, how can you tell whether the type of charge on them is the same or different?

15. Explain why the outside cases of electric appliances usually are made of plastic.

Developing Skills

16. **Classifying** Look at several objects around your home. Classify these objects as insulators or conductors.

17. Making and Using Graphs The following data show the current and voltage in a circuit containing a portable CD player and in a circuit containing a portable radio.

a. Make a graph with the horizontal axis as current and the vertical axis as voltage. Plot the data for both appliances.

b. Which line is more horizontal—the plot of the radio data or the CD player data?

c. Use Ohm's law to determine the electrical resistance of each device.

d. For which device is the line more horizontal—the device with the higher or lower resistance?

Portable Radio		Portable CD Player	
Voltage (V)	Current (A)	Voltage (V)	Current (A)
2.0	1.0	2.0	0.5
4.0	2.0	4.0	1.0
6.0	3.0	6.0	1.5

18. Collecting Data Determine the total cost of keeping all the lights turned on in your living room for 24 h if the cost of electricity is $0.08 per kilowatt-hour.

Performance Assessment

19. Design a Board Game Design a board game about a series or parallel circuit. The rules of the game could be based on opening or closing the circuit, adding fuses, and/or resetting a circuit breaker.

TECHNOLOGY

 Go to the Glencoe Science Web site at **science.glencoe.com** or use the **Glencoe Science CD-ROM** for additional chapter assessment.

THE PRINCETON REVIEW | **Test Practice**

A student is interested in setting up and comparing four different circuits. The table below lists her results.

Type of Electric Circuit			
Circuit	Number of Resistors	Circuit Type	Battery Voltage
A	2	Series	6 V
B	3	Parallel	12 V
C	4	Series	4 V
D	5	Parallel	8 V

Study the chart above and answer the following questions.

1. The voltage across a resistor in a parallel circuit equals the battery voltage. In a series circuit, the voltage across a resistor is less than the battery voltage. In which circuit is the voltage across an individual resistor the greatest?

A) Circuit A
B) Circuit B
C) Circuit C
D) Circuit D

2. A certain electric motor requires at least 5 volts to run. According to the table, the battery in which circuit could NOT be used to run the motor?

F) Circuit A
G) Circuit B
H) Circuit C
J) Circuit D

Magnetism

This maglev train is designed to travel at speeds up to 500 km/h. However, you won't see any steam or exhaust coming out of its engine. In fact this train is not even touching the track. That's because it is suspended by magnetic forces and propelled by a traveling magnetic field. In this chapter, you will learn why magnets attract certain materials. You will also learn how electricity and magnetism are connected, and how an electric current can create a magnetic field.

What do you think?

Science Journal Look at the picture below with a classmate. Discuss what is happening. Here's a hint: *No glue or tape is involved.* Write your answer or best guess in your Science Journal.

Perhaps you've driven bumper cars with your friends, and remember the jolt you felt when you crashed into another car. Quite a force can be generated from that small car powered by an electric motor. How does the motor produce a force that gets the tires moving? The answer involves magnetism. The following activity will demonstrate how a magnet is able to exert forces.

Observe and measure force between magnets

1. Place two bar magnets on opposite ends of a sheet of paper.

2. Slowly slide one magnet toward the other until it moves. Measure the distance between the magnets.

3. Turn one magnet around 180°. Repeat the activity. Then turn the other magnet and repeat again.

4. Repeat the activity with one magnet perpendicular to the other, in a T shape.

Observe

In your Science Journal, record your results. In each case, how close did the magnets have to be to affect each other? Did the magnets move together or apart? How did the forces exerted by the magnets change as the magnets were moved closer together? Explain.

Before You Read

FOLDABLES
Reading & Study
Skills

Making a Compare and Contrast Study Fold Make the following Foldable to help you see how magnetic forces and magnetic fields are similar and different.

1. Place a sheet of paper in front of you so the long side is at the top. Fold the paper in half from the left side to the right side. Unfold.

2. Fold each side in to the fold line to divide the paper into fourths.

3. Label the flaps *Magnetic Force* and *Magnetic Field*.

4. As you read the chapter, write information about each topic on the inside of each flap.

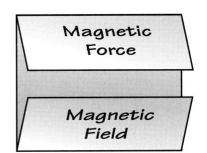

1 What is magnetism?

Early Uses

Do you use magnets to attach papers to a metal surface such as a refrigerator? Have you ever wondered why magnets and some metals attract? Thousands of years ago, people noticed that a mineral called magnetite attracted other pieces of magnetite and bits of iron. They discovered that when they rubbed small pieces of iron with magnetite, the iron began to act like magnetite. When these pieces were free to turn, one end pointed north. These might have been the first compasses. The compass was an important development for navigation and exploration, especially at sea. Before compasses, sailors had to depend on the Sun or the stars to know in which direction they were going.

Magnets

A piece of magnetite is a magnet. Magnets attract objects made of iron or steel, such as nails and paper clips. Magnets also can attract or repel other magnets. Every magnet has two ends, or poles. One end is called the north pole and the other is the south pole. As shown in **Figure 1,** a north magnetic pole always repels other north poles and always attracts south poles. Likewise, a south pole always repels other south poles and attracts north poles.

Figure 1
Two north poles or two south poles repel each other. North and south magnetic poles are attracted to each other.

Two north poles repel

Two south poles repel

Opposite poles attract

The Magnetic Field You have to handle a pair of magnets for only a short time before you can feel that magnets attract or repel without touching each other. How can a magnet cause an object to move without touching it? Recall that a force is a push or a pull that can cause an object to move. Just like gravitational and electric forces, a magnetic force can be exerted even when objects are not touching. And like these forces, the magnetic force becomes weaker as the magnets get farther apart. This magnetic force is exerted through a **magnetic field.** Magnetic fields surround all magnets. If you sprinkle iron filings near a magnet, the iron filings will outline the magnetic field around the magnet. Take a look at **Figure 2A.** The iron filings form a pattern of curved lines that start on one pole and end on the other. These curved lines are called magnetic field lines. Magnetic field lines help show the direction of the magnetic field.

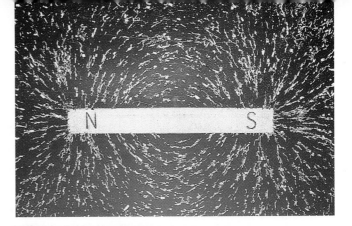

 **A** Iron filings show the magnetic field lines around a bar magnet.

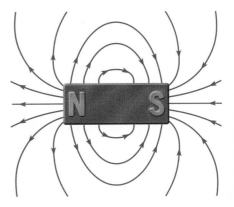

B Magnetic field lines start at the north pole of the magnet and end on the south pole.

Reading Check *What is the evidence that a magnetic field exists?*

Magnetic field lines begin at a magnet's north pole and end on the south pole, as shown in **Figure 2B.** The field lines are close together where the field is strong and get farther apart as the field gets weaker. As you can see in the figures, the magnetic field is strongest close to the magnetic poles and grows weaker farther from the poles.

Field lines that curve toward each other show attraction. Field lines that curve away from each other show repulsion. **Figure 3** illustrates the magnetic field lines between a north and a south pole and the field lines between two north poles.

Figure 2
A magnetic field surrounds a magnet. Where the magnetic field lines are close together, the field is strong. *For this magnet, where is the field strongest?*

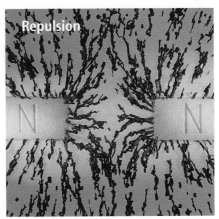

Figure 3
Magnetic field lines show attraction and repulsion. *What would the field between two south poles look like?*

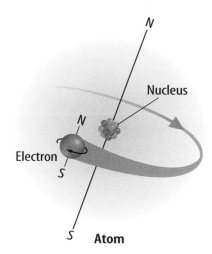

Figure 4
Movement of electrons produces magnetic fields. *What are the two types of motion shown in the illustration?*

Figure 5
Some materials can become temporary magnets.

Making Magnetic Fields A magnet is surrounded by a magnetic field that enables the magnet to exert a magnetic force. How are magnetic fields made? A moving electric charge creates a magnetic field.

Inside every magnet are moving charges. All atoms contain negatively charged particles called electrons. Not only do these electrons swarm around the nucleus of an atom, they also spin, as shown in **Figure 4.** Because of its movement, each electron produces a magnetic field. The atoms that make up magnets have their electrons arranged so that each atom is like a small magnet. In a material such as iron, a large number of atoms will have their magnetic fields pointing in the same direction. This group of atoms, with their fields pointing in the same direction, is called a **magnetic domain.**

A material that can become magnetized, such as iron or steel, contains many magnetic domains. When the material is not magnetized, these domains are oriented in different directions, as shown in **Figure 5A.** The magnetic fields created by the domains cancel, so the material does not act like a magnet.

A magnet contains a large number of magnetic domains that are lined up and pointing in the same direction. Suppose a strong magnet is held close to a material such as iron or steel. The magnet causes the magnetic field in many magnetic domains to line up with the magnet's field, as shown in **Figure 5B.** As you can see in **Figure 5C** this process magnetizes paper clips.

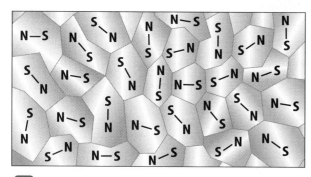

A Microscopic sections of iron and steel act as tiny magnets. Normally, these domains are oriented randomly and their magnetic fields cancel each other.

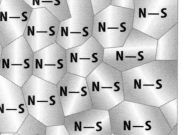

B When a strong magnet is brought near the material, the domains line up, and their magnetic fields add together.

C The bar magnet magnetizes the paper clips. The top of each paper clip is now a north pole, and the bottom is a south pole.

Earth's Magnetic Field

Magnetism isn't limited to bar magnets. Earth has a magnetic field, as shown in **Figure 6.** The region of space affected by Earth's magnetic field is called the **magnetosphere** (mag NEE tuh sfihr). The origin of Earth's magnetic field is thought to be deep within Earth in the outer core layer. One theory is that movement of molten iron in the outer core is responsible for generating Earth's magnetic field. The shape of Earth's magnetic field is similar to that of a huge bar magnet tilted about 11° from Earth's geographic north and south poles.

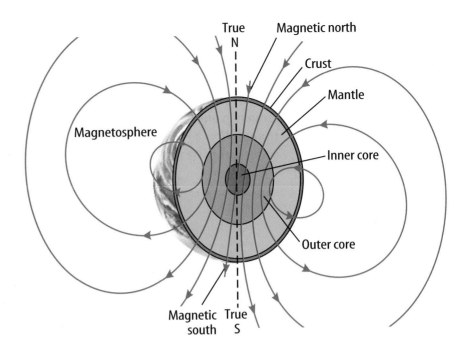

Figure 6
Earth has a magnetic field similar to the field of a bar magnet.

Problem-Solving Activity

Finding the Magnetic Declination

The north pole of a compass points toward the magnetic pole, rather than true north. Imagine drawing a line between your location and the north pole, and a line between your location and the magnetic pole. The angle between these two lines is called the magnetic declination. Sometimes knowing the magnetic declination can be important if you need to know the direction to true north, rather than to the magnetic pole. However, the magnetic declination changes depending on your position.

Identifying the Problem

Suppose your location is at 50° N and 110° W. You wish to head true north. The location of the north pole is at 90° N and 110° W, and the location of the magnetic pole is at about 80° N and

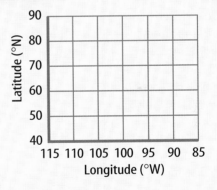

105° W. What is the magnetic declination angle at your location?

Solving the Problem

1. Label a graph like the one shown above.
2. On the graph, plot your location, the location of the magnetic pole, and the location of the north pole.
3. Draw a line from your location to the north pole, and a line from your location to the magnetic pole.
4. Using a protractor measure the angle between the two lines.

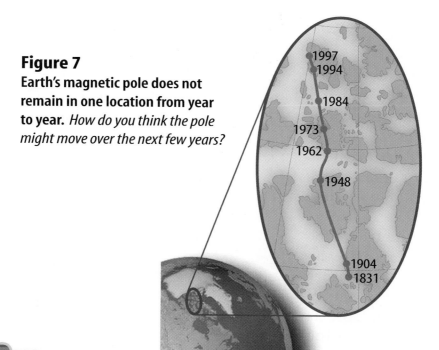

Figure 7
Earth's magnetic pole does not remain in one location from year to year. *How do you think the pole might move over the next few years?*

1997
1994
1984
1973
1962
1948
1904
1831

Mini LAB

Observing Magnetic Fields

Procedure
1. Place **iron filings** in a **plastic petri dish.** Cover the dish and **tape** it closed.
2. Collect **several magnets.** Place the magnets on the table and hold the dish over each one. Draw a diagram of what happens to the filings in each case.
3. Arrange two or more magnets under the dish. Observe the pattern of the filings.

Analysis
1. What happens to the filings close to the poles? Far from the poles?
2. Compare the fields of the individual magnets. How can you tell which magnet is strongest? Weakest?

Life Science INTEGRATION

Nature's Magnets Honeybees, rainbow trout, and homing pigeons have something in common with sailors and hikers. They take advantage of magnetism to find their way. Instead of using compasses, these animals and others have tiny pieces of magnetite in their bodies. These pieces are so small that they may contain a single magnetic domain. Scientists have shown that some animals use these natural magnets to detect Earth's magnetic field. They appear to use Earth's magnetic field, along with other clues like the position of the Sun or stars, to help them navigate.

Earth's Changing Magnetic Field Earth's magnetic poles do not stay in one place. The magnetic pole in the north today, as shown in **Figure 7,** is in a different place from where it was 20 years ago. In fact, not only does the position of the magnetic poles move, but Earth's magnetic field sometimes reverses direction. For example, 700 thousand years ago, a compass needle that now points north would point south. During the past 20 million years, Earth's magnetic field has reversed direction more than 70 times. The magnetism of ancient rocks contains a record of these magnetic field changes. When some types of molten rock cool, magnetic domains of iron in the rock line up with Earth's magnetic field. After the rock cools, the orientation of these domains is frozen into position. Consequently, these old rocks preserve the orientation of Earth's magnetic field as it was long ago.

Figure 8
The compass needles align with the magnetic field lines around the magnet. *What happens to the compass needles when the bar magnet is removed?*

The Compass How can humans detect and measure Earth's magnetic field? The compass is a useful tool for finding and mapping magnetic fields. A compass has a needle that is free to turn. The needle itself is a small magnet with a north and a south magnetic pole. A magnet placed close to a compass causes the needle to rotate until it is aligned with the magnetic field line that passes through the compass, as shown in **Figure 8.**

Earth's magnetic field also causes a compass needle to rotate. The north pole of the compass needle points toward Earth's magnetic pole that is near the geographic north pole. Unlike poles attract, so this magnetic pole is actually a magnetic south pole. Earth's magnetic field is like that of a bar magnet with the magnet's south pole near Earth's north pole.

SCIENCE *Online*

Research A compass needle doesn't point directly toward the north. How much the needle is offset from the north varies from place to place. Visit the Glencoe Science Web site at **science.glencoe.com** to find out where the compass points in your location.

Section ① Assessment

1. Why do atoms behave like magnets?
2. Explain why magnets attract iron but do not attract paper.
3. How is the behavior of electric charges similar to that of magnetic poles?
4. Around a magnet, where is the field the strongest? Where is it the weakest?
5. **Think Critically** A horseshoe magnet is a bar magnet bent into the shape of the letter U. When would two horseshoe magnets attract each other? Repel? Have little effect?

Skill Builder Activities

6. **Comparing and Contrasting** Compare and contrast the three phenomena of *gravity, electricity,* and *magnetism.* Use the terms *force* and *field* in your comparison. **For more help, refer to the** Science Skill Handbook.

7. **Communicating** Imagine you are an early explorer. In your Science Journal, explain how a compass would change your work. Describe the difficulties of working without a compass. **For more help, refer to the** Science Skill Handbook.

Activity

Make a Compass

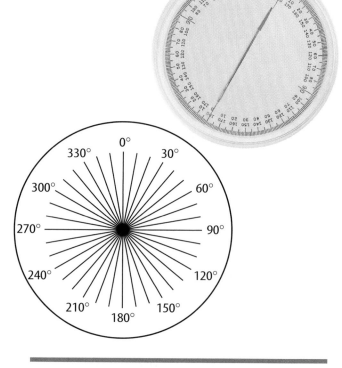

A valuable tool for hikers and campers is a compass. Almost 1,000 years ago, Chinese inventors found a way to magnetize pieces of iron. They used this method to manufacture compasses. You can use the same procedure to make a compass.

What You'll Investigate
How do you construct a compass?

Materials
petri dish
*clear bowl
water
sewing needle
magnet

tape
marker
paper
plastic spoon
*Alternate material

Goals
- **Observe** induced magnetism.
- **Build** a compass.

Safety

Procedure

1. Reproduce the circular protractor shown. Tape it under the bottom of your dish so it can be seen but not get wet. Add water until the dish is half full.

2. Mark one end of the needle with a marker. Magnetize a needle by placing it on the magnet aligned north and south for 1 min.

3. Float the needle carefully in the dish. Use a plastic spoon to lower the needle onto the water. Turn the dish so the marked part of the needle is above the 0° mark. This is your compass.

4. Bring the magnet near your compass. Observe how the needle reacts. Measure the angle the needle turns.

Conclude and Apply

1. **Explain** why the marked end of the needle always pointed the same way in step 3, even though you rotated the dish.

2. **Describe** the behavior of the compass when the magnet was brought close.

3. Does the marked end of your needle point to the north or south pole of the bar magnet? Infer whether the marked end of your needle is a north or a south pole. How do you know?

Communicating Your Data

Make a half-page insert that will go into a wilderness survival guide to describe the procedure for making a compass. Share your half-page insert with your classmates. **For more help, refer to the** Science Skill Handbook.

Electricity and Magnetism

Current Can Make a Magnet

Magnetic fields are produced by moving electric charges. Electrons moving around the nuclei of atoms produce magnetic fields. The motion of these electrons causes some materials, such as iron, to be magnetic. You cause electric charges to move when you flip a light switch or turn on a portable CD player. When electric current flows in a wire, electric charges move in the wire. As a result, a wire that contains an electric current also is surrounded by a magnetic field. **Figure 9A** shows the magnetic field produced around a wire that carries an electric current.

Electromagnets Look at the magnetic field lines around the coils of wire in **Figure 9B.** The magnetic fields around each coil of wire add together to form a stronger magnetic field inside the coil. When the coils are wrapped around an iron core, the magnetic field of the coils magnetizes the iron. The iron then becomes a magnet, which adds to the strength of the magnetic field inside the coil. A current-carrying wire wrapped around an iron core is called an **electromagnet,** as shown in **Figure 9C.**

As You Read

What **You'll Learn**

■ **Describe** the relationship between electricity and magnetism.
■ **Explain** how electricity can produce motion.
■ **Explain** how motion can produce electricity.

Vocabulary

electromagnet   generator
motor   alternating current
aurora   transformer

Why **It's Important**

The electric current that comes from your wall socket is available because of magnetism.

Figure 9
A current-carrying wire produces a magnetic field.

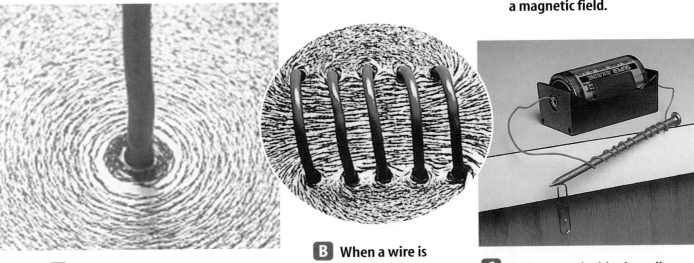

A Iron particles show the magnetic field lines around a current-carrying wire.

B When a wire is wrapped in a coil, the field inside the coil is made stronger.

C An iron core inside the coils increases the magnetic field because the core becomes magnetized.

Figure 10

An electric doorbell uses an electromagnet. Each time the electromagnet is turned on, the hammer strikes the bell. *How is the electromagnet turned off?*

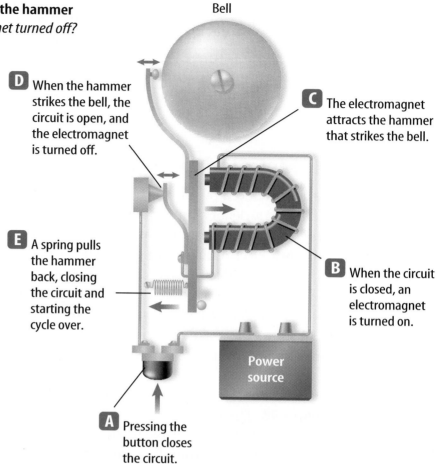

Bell

D When the hammer strikes the bell, the circuit is open, and the electromagnet is turned off.

C The electromagnet attracts the hammer that strikes the bell.

E A spring pulls the hammer back, closing the circuit and starting the cycle over.

B When the circuit is closed, an electromagnet is turned on.

Power source

A Pressing the button closes the circuit.

TRY AT HOME Mini LAB

Assembling an Electromagnet

Procedure 🥽 🧤 ✋

1. Wrap a **wire** around a **16-penny steel nail** ten times. Connect one end of the wire to a **D-cell battery,** as shown in **Figure 9C.** Leave the other end loose until you use the electromagnet. **WARNING:** *When current is flowing in the wire, it can become hot over time.*

2. Connect the wire. Observe how many **paper clips** you can pick up with the magnet.

3. Disconnect the wire and rewrap the nail with 20 coils. Connect the wire and observe how many paper clips you can pick up. Disconnect the wire again.

Analysis

1. How many paper clips did you pick up each time? Did more coils make the electromagnet stronger or weaker?

2. Graph the number of coils versus number of paper clips attracted. Predict how many paper clips would be picked up with five coils of wire. Check your prediction.

Using Electromagnets The magnetic field of an electromagnet is turned on or off when the electric current is turned on or off. By changing the current, the strength and direction of the magnetic field of an electromagnet can be changed. This has led to a number of practical uses for electromagnets. A doorbell, as shown in **Figure 10,** is a familiar use of an electromagnet. When you press the button by the door, you close a switch in a circuit that includes an electromagnet. The magnet attracts an iron bar attached to a hammer. The hammer strikes the bell. When the hammer strikes the bell, the hammer has moved far enough to open the circuit again. The electromagnet loses its magnetic field, and a spring pulls the iron bar and hammer back into place. This movement closes the circuit, and the cycle is repeated as long as the button is pushed.

Some gauges, such as the gas gauge in a car, use a galvanometer to move the gauge pointer. **Figure 11** shows how a galvanometer makes a pointer move. Ammeters and voltmeters used to measure current and voltage in electric circuits also use galvanometers, as shown in **Figure 11.**

VISUALIZING VOLTMETERS AND AMMETERS

Figure 11

The gas gauge in a car uses a device called a galvanometer to make the needle of the gauge move. Galvanometers are also used in other measuring devices. A voltmeter uses a galvanometer to measure the voltage in a electric circuit. An ammeter uses a galvanometer to measure electric current. Multimeters can be used as an ammeter or voltmeter by turning a switch.

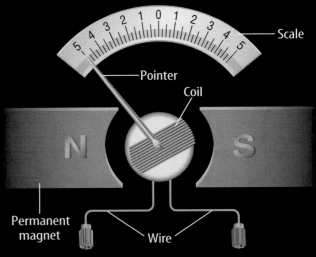

A galvanometer has a pointer attached to a coil that can rotate between the poles of a permanent magnet. When a current flows through the coil, it becomes an electromagnet. Attraction and repulsion between the magnetic poles of the electromagnet and the poles of the permanent magnet makes the coil rotate. The amount of rotation depends on the amount of current in the coil.

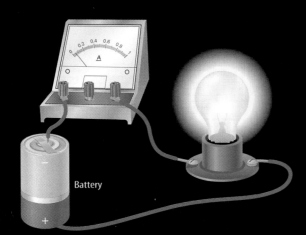

To measure the current in a circuit an ammeter is used. An ammeter contains a galvanometer and has low resistance. To measure current, an ammeter is connected in series in the circuit, so all the current in the circuit flows through it. The greater the current in the circuit, the more the needle moves.

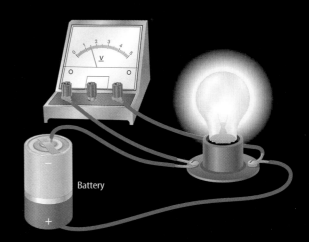

To measure the voltage in a circuit a voltmeter is used. A voltmeter also contains a galvanometer and has high resistance. To measure voltage, a voltmeter is connected in parallel in the circuit, so almost no current flows through it. The higher the voltage in the circuit, the more the needle moves.

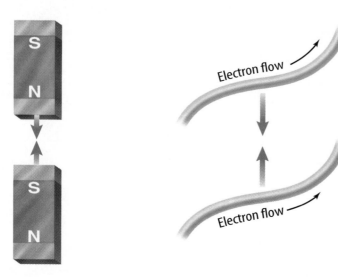

Magnets Push and Pull Currents

Look around for electric appliances that produce motion, such as a fan. How does the electric energy entering the fan become transformed into the kinetic energy of the moving fan blades? Recall that current-carrying wires produce a magnetic field. This magnetic field behaves the same way as the magnetic field that a magnet produces. Two current-carrying wires can attract each other as if they were two magnets, as shown in **Figure 12.**

Figure 12

Two wires carrying current in the same direction attract each other, just as unlike magnetic poles do.

Electric Motor Just as two magnets exert a force on each other, a magnet and a current-carrying wire exert forces on each other. The magnetic field around a current-carrying wire will cause it to be pushed or pulled by a magnet, depending on the direction the current is flowing in the wire. As a result, some of the electric energy carried by the current is converted into kinetic energy of the moving wire, as shown in **Figure 13A.** Any device that converts electric energy into kinetic energy is a **motor.** To keep a motor running, the current-carrying wire is formed into a loop so the magnetic field can force the wire to spin continually, as shown in **Figure 13B.**

Figure 13

In an electric motor, the force a magnet exerts on a current-carrying wire transforms electric energy into kinetic energy.

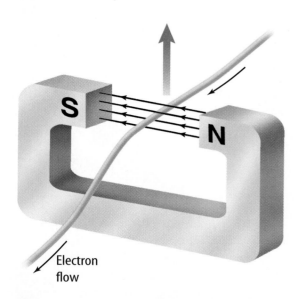

A A magnetic field like the one shown will push a current-carrying wire upward.

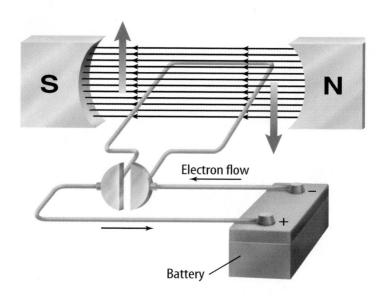

B The magnetic field exerts a force on the wire loop, causing it to spin as long as current flows in the loop.

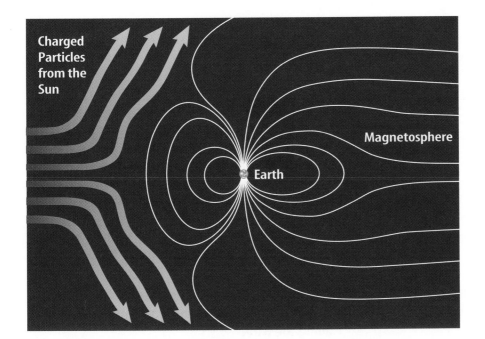

Figure 14
Earth's magnetosphere deflects most of the charged particles streaming from the Sun. *Why is the magnetosphere stretched away from the Sun?*

Earth's Magnetosphere The Sun emits charged particles that stream through the solar system like an enormous electric current. Just like a current-carrying wire is pushed or pulled by a magnetic field, Earth's magnetic field pushes and pulls on the electric current generated by the Sun. This causes most of the charged particles in this current to be deflected so they never strike Earth, as shown in **Figure 14.** As a result, living things on Earth are protected from damage that might be caused by these charged particles. At the same time, the solar current pushes on Earth's magnetosphere so it is stretched away from the Sun.

The Aurora Sometimes the Sun ejects a large number of charged particles all at once. Most of these charged particles are deflected by Earth's magnetosphere. However, some of the ejected particles from the Sun produce other charged particles in Earth's outer atmosphere. These charged particles spiral along Earth's magnetic field lines toward Earth's magnetic poles. There they collide with atoms in the atmosphere. These collisions cause the atoms to emit light. The light emitted causes a display known as the **aurora** (uh ROR uh), as shown in **Figure 15.** In northern latitudes, the aurora sometimes is called the northern lights.

Figure 15
An aurora is a natural light show that occurs in the southern and northern skies.

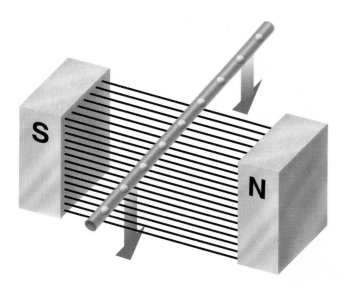

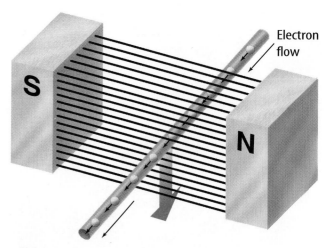

Electron flow

A If a wire is pulled through a magnetic field, the electrons in the wire also move downward.

B The magnetic field then exerts a force on the moving electrons, causing them to move along the wire.

Figure 16
When a wire is made to move through a magnetic field, an electric current can be produced in the wire.

Figure 17
In a generator, a power source spins a wire loop in a magnetic field. Every half turn, the current will reverse direction. This type of generator supplies alternating current to the lightbulb.

Using Magnets to Create Current

In an electric motor, a magnetic field turns electricity into motion. A device called a **generator** uses a magnetic field to turn motion into electricity. Electric motors and electric generators both involve conversions between electric energy and kinetic energy. In a motor, electric energy is changed into kinetic energy. In a generator, kinetic energy is changed into electric energy. **Figure 16** shows how a current can be produced in a wire that moves in a magnetic field. As the wire moves, the electrons in the wire also move in the same direction, as shown in **Figure 16A.** The magnetic field exerts a force on the moving electrons that pushes them along the wire, as shown in **Figure 16B,** creating an electric current.

Electric Generators To produce electric current, the wire is fashioned into a loop, as in **Figure 17.** A power source provides the kinetic energy to spin the wire loop. With each half turn, the current in the loop changes direction. This causes the current to alternate from positive to negative. Such a current is called an **alternating current** (AC). In the United States, electric currents change from positive to negative to positive 60 times each second.

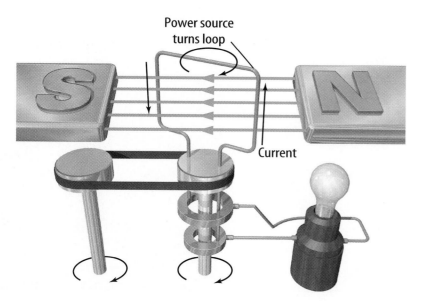

Power source turns loop

Current

Types of Current A battery produces direct current instead of alternating current. In a direct current (DC) electrons flow in one direction. In an alternating current, electrons change their direction of movement many times each second. Some generators are built to produce direct current instead of alternating current.

✔ **Reading Check** *What type of currents can be produced by a generator?*

Power Plants Electric generators produce almost all of the electric energy used all over the world. Small generators can produce energy for one household, and large generators in electric power plants can provide electric energy for thousands of homes. Different energy sources such as gas, coal, and water are used to provide the kinetic energy to rotate coils of wire in a magnetic field. Coal-burning power plants, like the one pictured in **Figure 18,** are the most common. More than half of the electric energy generated by power plants in the United States comes from burning coal.

Voltage The electric energy produced at a power plant is carried to your home in wires. Recall that voltage is a measure of how much energy the electric charges in a current are carrying. The electric transmission lines from electric power plants transmit electric energy at a high voltage of about 700,000 V. Transmitting electric energy at a low voltage is less efficient because more electric energy is converted into heat in the wires. However, high voltage is not safe for use in homes and businesses. A device is needed to reduce the voltage.

SCIENCE *Online*

Research Visit the Glencoe Science Web site at **science.glencoe.com** for more information about the different types of power plants used in your region of the country. Communicate to your class what you learn.

Figure 18
Coal-burning power plants supply much of the electric energy for the world.

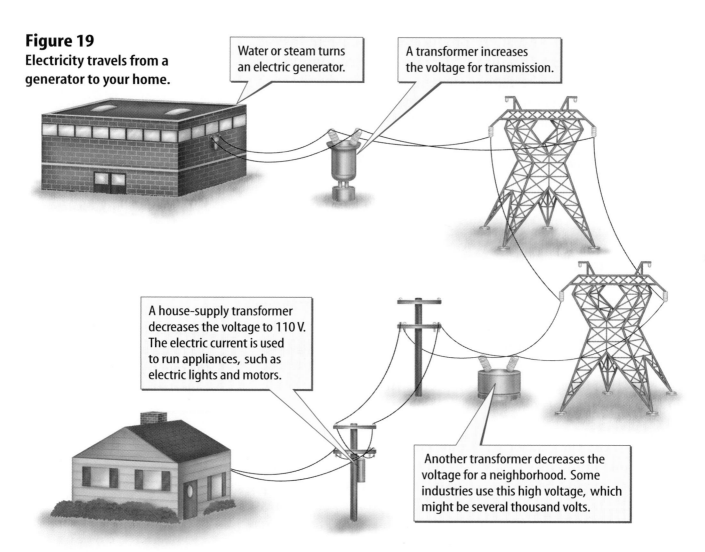

Figure 19
Electricity travels from a generator to your home.

Water or steam turns an electric generator.

A transformer increases the voltage for transmission.

A house-supply transformer decreases the voltage to 110 V. The electric current is used to run appliances, such as electric lights and motors.

Another transformer decreases the voltage for a neighborhood. Some industries use this high voltage, which might be several thousand volts.

Changing Voltage

A **transformer** is a device that changes the voltage of an alternating current with little loss of energy. Transformers are used to increase the voltage before transmitting an electric current through the power lines. Other transformers are used to decrease the voltage to the level needed for home or industrial use. Such a power system is shown in **Figure 19.** Transformers also are used in power adaptors. For battery-operated devices, a power adaptor must change the 110 V from the wall outlet to the same voltage produced by the device's batteries.

Reading Check *What does a transformer do?*

A transformer usually has two coils of wire wrapped around an iron core, as shown in **Figure 20.** One coil is connected to an alternating current source. The current creates a magnetic field in the iron core, just like in an electromagnet. Because the current is alternating, the magnetic field it produces also switches direction. This alternating magnetic field in the core then causes an alternating current in the other wire coil.

Figure 20
A transformer can increase or decrease voltage. The ratio of input coils to output coils equals the ratio of input voltage to output voltage. *If the input voltage here is 60 V, what is the output voltage?*

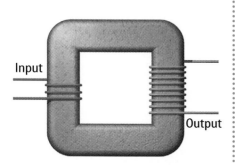

Input

Output

The Transformer Ratio Whether a transformer increases or decreases the input voltage depends on the number of coils on each side of the transformer. The ratio of the number of coils on the input side to the number of coils on the output side is the same as the ratio of the input voltage to the output voltage. For the transformer in **Figure 20** the ratio of the number of coils on the input side to the number of coils on the output side is three to nine, or one to three. If the input voltage is 60 V, the output voltage will be 180 V.

In a transformer the voltage is greater on the side with more coils. If the number of coils on the input side is greater than the number of coils on the output side, the voltage is decreased. If the number of coils on the input side is less than the number on the output side, the voltage is increased.

Superconductors

Electric current can flow easily through materials, such as metals, that are electrical conductors. However, even in conductors, there is some resistance to this flow and heat is produced as electrons collide with atoms in the material.

Unlike an electrical conductor, a material known as a superconductor has no resistance to the flow of electrons. Superconductors are formed when certain materials are cooled to low temperatures. For example, aluminum becomes a superconductor at about −272°C. When an electric current flows through a superconductor, no heat is produced and no electric energy is converted into heat.

Figure 21
A small magnet floats above a superconductor. The magnet causes the superconductor to produce a magnetic field that repels the magnet.

Superconductors and Magnets Superconductors also have other unusual properties. For example, a magnet is repelled by a superconductor. As the magnet gets close to the superconductor, the superconductor creates a magnetic field that is opposite to the field of the magnet. The field created by the superconductor can cause the magnet to float above it, as shown in **Figure 21.**

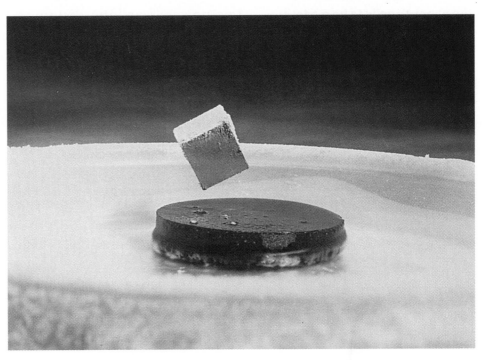

Figure 22
The particle accelerator at Fermi National Accelerator Laboratory near Batavia, Illinois, accelerates atomic particles to nearly the speed of light. The particles travel in a beam only a few millimeters in diameter. Magnets made of superconductors keep the beam moving in a circular path about 2 km in diameter.

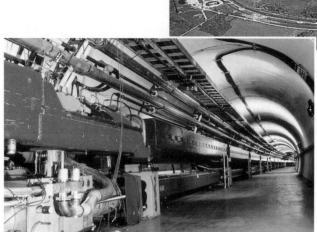

Figure 23
A patient is being placed inside an MRI machine. The strong magnetic field inside the machine enables images of tissues inside the patient's body to be made.

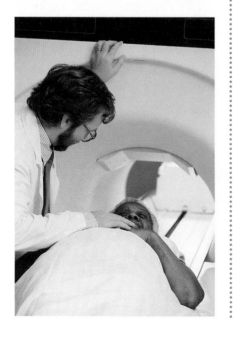

Using Superconductors Large electric currents can flow through electromagnets made from superconducting wire and can produce extremely strong magnetic fields. The particle accelerator shown in **Figure 22** uses more than 1,000 superconducting electromagnets to help accelerate subatomic particles to nearly the speed of light.

Other uses for superconductors are being developed. Transmission lines made from a superconductor could transmit electric power over long distances without having any electric energy converted to heat. It also may be possible to construct extremely fast computers using microchips made from superconductor materials.

Magnetic Resonance Imaging

A method called magnetic resonance imaging, or MRI, uses magnetic fields to create images of the inside of a human body. MRI images can show if tissue is damaged or diseased, and can detect the presence of tumors.

Unlike X-ray imaging, which uses X-ray radiation that can damage tissue, MRI uses a strong magnetic field and radio waves. The patient is placed inside a machine like the one shown in **Figure 23.** Inside the machine an electromagnet made from superconductor materials produces a magnetic field more than 20,000 times stronger than Earth's magnetic field.

Producing MRI Images About 63 percent of all the atoms in your body are hydrogen atoms. The nucleus of a hydrogen atom is a proton, which behaves like a tiny magnet. The strong magnetic field inside the MRI tube causes these protons to line up along the direction of the field. Radio waves are then applied to the part of the body being examined. The protons absorb some of the energy in the radio waves, and change the direction of their alignment.

When the radio waves are turned off, the protons realign themselves with the magnetic field and emit the energy they absorbed. The amount of energy emitted depends on the type of tissue in the body. This energy emitted is detected and a computer uses this information to form an image, like the one shown in **Figure 24.**

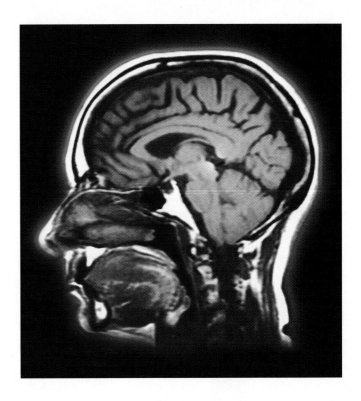

Figure 24
This MRI image shows a side view of the brain. An MRI scan can produce images from several angles, as well as cross-sections.

Connecting Electricity and Magnetism Electric forces and magnetic forces are similar in some ways. Both forces can repel or attract. Like electric charges repel each other, and like magnetic poles repel each other. Positive and negative electric charges attract, and north and south magnetic poles attract.

Electric charges and magnets are connected in another important way. Moving electric charges produce magnetic fields, and magnetic fields exert forces on moving electric charges. It is this connection enables electric motors and generators to operate.

Section Assessment

1. What is an electromagnet? How can you make one in the classroom?

2. How does a transformer work?

3. How does a magnetic field affect a current-carrying wire?

4. How does a generator turn motion into electrical energy?

5. **Think Critically** How is an electric motor similar to an aurora? Use the terms current, field, and kinetic energy in your answer.

Skill Builder Activities

6. **Researching Information** Research the types of power plants in your state. Make a poster showing the fuels that are used. **For more help, refer to the** Science Skill Handbook.

7. **Calculating Ratios** A transformer has ten turns of wire on the input side and 50 turns of wire on the output side. If the input voltage is 120 V, what will the output voltage be? **For more help, refer to the** Math Skill Handbook.

Activity

How does an electric motor work?

Electric motors are used in many appliances. For example, a computer contains a cooling fan and motors to spin the hard drive. A CD player contains electric motors to spin the CD. Some cars contain electric motors that move windows up and down, change the position of the seats, and blow warm or cold air into the car's interior. All these electric motors consist of an electromagnet and a permanent magnet. In this activity you will build a simple electric motor that will work for you.

What You'll Investigate

How can you change electric energy into motion?

Goals
- **Assemble** a small electric motor.
- **Observe** how the motor works.

Safety Precautions

Hold only the insulated part of each wire when they are attached to the battery. Use care when hammering the nails. After cutting the wire, the ends will be sharp.

Materials
22-gauge enameled wire (4 m)
steel knitting needle
*steel rod
nails (4)
hammer
ceramic magnets (2)
18-gauge insulated wire (60 cm)
masking tape
fine sandpaper
approximately 15-cm wooden board
wooden blocks (2)
6-V battery
*1.5-V batteries connected in a series (4)
wire cutters
*scissors
*Alternate materials

Procedure

1. Use sandpaper to strip the enamel from about 4 cm of each end of the 22-gauge wire.

2. Leaving the stripped ends free, make this wire into a tight coil of at least 30 turns. A D-cell battery or a film canister will help in forming the coil. Tape the coil so it doesn't unravel.

3. Insert the knitting needle through the coil. Center the coil on the needle. Pull the wire's two ends to one end of the needle.

4. Near the ends of the wire, wrap masking tape around the needle to act as insulation. Then tape one bare wire to each side of the needle at the spot where the masking tape is.

5. Tape a ceramic magnet to each block so that a north pole extends from one and a south pole from the other.

6. Make the motor. Tap the nails into the wood block as shown in the figure. Try to cross the nails at the same height as the magnets so the coil will be suspended between them.

7. Place the needle on the nails. Use bits of wood or folded paper to adjust the positions of the magnets until the coil is directly between the magnets. The magnets should be as close to the coil as possible without touching it.

8. Cut two 30-cm lengths of 18-gauge wire. Use sandpaper to strip the ends of both wires. Attach one wire to each terminal of the battery. Holding only the insulated part of each wire, place one wire against each of the bare wires taped to the needle to close the circuit. Observe what happens.

Conclude and Apply

1. **Describe** what happens when you close the circuit by connecting the wires. Were the results expected?

2. **Describe** what happens when you open the circuit.

3. **Predict** what would happen if you used twice as many coils of wire.

*C*ommunicating

Your Data

Compare your conclusions with other students in your class. **For more help, refer to the** Science Skill Handbook.

"Aagjuuk[1] and Sivulliit[2]"
from Intellectual Culture of the Copper Eskimos
by Knud Rasmussen, told by Tatilgak

Respond to the Reading

1. How can you tell the importance of constellations to the Inuit for telling direction?

2. How is it possible that the Inuit could see the constellations in the morning sky?

The following are "magic words" that are spoken before the Inuit (IH noo wut) people go seal hunting. Inuit are native people that live in the arctic region. Because the Inuit live in relative darkness for much of the winter, they have learned to find their way by looking at the stars to guide them.

The verse below was collected by an ethnographer. An enthnographer studies the practices and beliefs of people in different cultures. The poem is about two constellations that are important to the Inuit people because their appearance marks the end of winter when the Sun begins to appear in the sky again.

By which way, I wonder the mornings—
You dear morning, get up!
See I am up!
By which way, I wonder,
the constellation *Aagjuuk* rises up in the sky?
By this way—perhaps—by the morning
It rises up!

Morning, you dear morning, get up!
See I am up!
By which way, I wonder,
the constellation *Sivulliit*
Has risen to the sky?
By this way—perhaps—by the morning.
It rises up!

[1]Inuit name for the constellation of stars called Aquila (A kwuh luh)
[2]Inuit name for the constellation of stars called Bootes (boh OH teez)

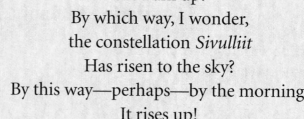

Understanding Literature

Ethnography Ethnography is a description of a culture. To write an ethnography, an ethnographer collects cultural stories, poems, or other oral tales from the culture that he or she is studying. Ethnographies of the Inuit are full of stories about the stars and constellations, but other forms of navigation are also important to the Inuit. It is important for the Inuit to be skilled in navigation because they must travel over vast areas of frozen ground that has few landmarks. The Inuit use other clues to navigate such as wind direction, sea currents, snowdrifts, and clouds.

Science Connection In this chapter you learned that Earth has a magnetic field. Earth's magnetic field causes the north pole of a compass needle to point in a northerly direction. Using a compass helps a person to navigate and find his or her way. However, at the far northern latitudes where the Inuit live, a compass becomes more difficult to use. Some Inuit live north of Earth's northern magnetic pole. In these locations a compass needle points in a southerly direction. As a result, the Inuit developed other ways to navigate.

Linking Science and Writing

Expository Writing Pretend your family is traveling from St. Louis, Missouri, to Madison, Wisconsin, on a summer evening. Use the library or the Internet to research the constellations in the summer sky in North America. Then write a paragraph describing the constellations that will help you and your family navigate north toward Wisconsin.

Career Connection

Astrophysicist

France Anne Cordova is familiar with the properties of gravity and magnetism in her innovative work with telescopes. Cordova was born in Paris, France to a Mexican American diplomat and grew up in California taking care of her 11 brothers and sisters. As a college student she became inspired by the first *Apollo* space mission and went on to earn a Ph.D. in physics from the California Institute of Technology. She was one of only two women in her graduating class. Cordova now serves as the vice chancellor for research at the University of California at Santa Barbara.

SCIENCE*Online* To learn more about careers in astrophysics, visit the Glencoe Science Web site at **science.glencoe.com**.

Reviewing Main Ideas

Section 1   What is magnetism?

1. All magnets have two poles—north and south. Like poles repel each other and unlike poles attract.

2. Electrons act like tiny magnets. Groups of atoms can align to form magnetic domains. If domains align, then a magnet is formed. *Why do magnets stick to some objects, such as refrigerators, but not others?*

3. A magnetic force acts through a magnetic field. Magnetic fields extend through space and point from a north pole to a south pole.

4. Earth has a magnetic field that can be detected using a compass. *What might be the cause for these green and red lights above Earth in the photo taken from the space shuttle in orbit?*

Section 2   Electricity and Magnetism

1. Electric current creates a magnetic field. Electromagnets are made from a coil of wire that carries a current, wrapped around an iron core. *How is this crane able to lift the scrap iron particles?*

2. A magnetic field exerts a force on a moving charge or a current-carrying wire.

3. Motors transform electric energy into kinetic energy. Generators transform kinetic energy into electric energy.

4. Transformers are used to increase and decrease voltage in AC circuits. *In this step-down transformer, which has more turns, the input coil or the output coil?*

FOLDABLES
Reading & Study
Skills

After You Read

Using the information on your Foldable, compare and contrast the terms *magnetic force* and *magnetic field.* Write your observations under the flaps in your Foldable.

Visualizing Main Ideas

Complete the following concept map.

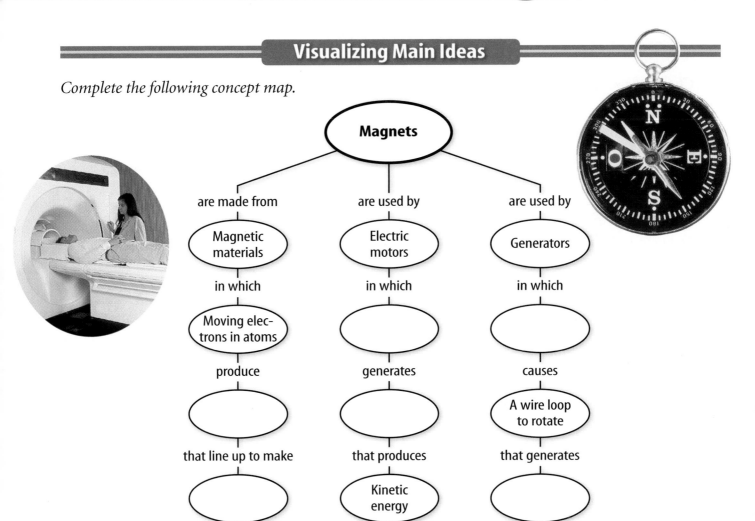

Magnets

are made from → Magnetic materials → in which → Moving electrons in atoms → produce → ( ) → that line up to make → ( )

are used by → Electric motors → in which → ( ) → generates → ( ) → that produces → Kinetic energy

are used by → Generators → in which → ( ) → causes → A wire loop to rotate → that generates → ( )

Vocabulary Review

Vocabulary Words

a. alternating current
b. aurora
c. electromagnet
d. generator
e. magnetic domain
f. magnetic field
g. magnetosphere
h. motor
i. transformer

THE PRINCETON REVIEW **Study Tip**

Look for examples in your home of what you are studying in science class. For instance, where can you find electric motors in your home?

Using Vocabulary

Explain the relationship that exists between each set of vocabulary words below.

1. generator, transformer
2. magnetic force, magnetic field
3. alternating current, direct current
4. current, electromagnet
5. motor, generator
6. electron, magnetism
7. magnetosphere, aurora
8. magnet, magnetic domain

Checking Concepts

Choose the word or phrase that best answers the question.

1. What can iron filings be used to show?
   A) magnetic field
   C) gravitational field
   B) electric field
   D) none of these

2. Why does the needle of a compass point to magnetic north?
   A) Earth's north pole is strongest.
   B) Earth's north pole is closest.
   C) Only the north pole attracts compasses.
   D) The compass needle aligns itself with Earth's magnetic field.

3. What will the north poles of two bar magnets do when brought together?
   A) attract
   B) create an electric current
   C) repel
   D) not interact

4. How many poles do all magnets have?
   A) one
   C) three
   B) two
   D) one or two

5. When a current-carrying wire is wrapped around an iron core, what can it create?
   A) an aurora
   C) a generator
   B) a magnet
   D) a motor

6. What does a transformer between utility wires and your house do?
   A) increases voltage
   B) decreases voltage
   C) leaves voltage the same
   D) changes DC to AC

7. Which energy transformation occurs in an electric motor?
   A) electrical to kinetic
   B) electrical to thermal
   C) potential to kinetic
   D) kinetic to electrical

8. What prevents most charged particles from the Sun from hitting Earth?
   A) the aurora
   B) Earth's magnetic field
   C) high-altitude electric fields
   D) Earth's atmosphere

9. Which of these objects do magnetic fields NOT interact with?
   A) magnets
   C) current
   B) steel
   D) paper

10. Which energy transformation occurs in an electric generator?
    A) electrical to kinetic
    B) electrical to thermal
    C) potential to kinetic
    D) kinetic to electrical

Thinking Critically

11. Why don't ordinary bar magnets line themselves up with Earth's magnetic field when you set them on a table?

12. If you were given a magnet with unmarked poles, how could you determine which pole was which?

13. A nail is magnetized by holding the south pole of a magnet against the head of the nail. Is the point of the nail a north or a south pole? Sketch your explanation.

14. If you add more coils to an electromagnet, does the magnet get stronger or weaker? Why? What happens if the current increases?

15. What are the sources of magnetic fields? How can you demonstrate this?

Developing Skills

16. **Identifying and Manipulating Variables and Controls** How could you test and compare the strength of two different magnets?

17. **Forming Operational Definitions** Give an operational definition of an electromagnet.

18. **Concept Mapping** Explain how a doorbell uses an electromagnet by placing the following phrases in the cycle concept map: *circuit open, circuit closed, electromagnet turned on, electromagnet turned off, hammer attracted to magnet and strikes bell,* and *hammer pulled back by a spring.*

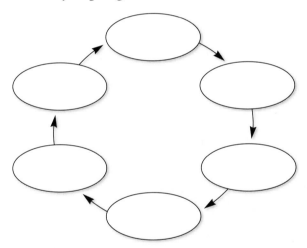

Performance Assessment

19. **Multimedia Presentation** Prepare a multimedia presentation to inform your classmates on the future uses of magnets and magnetism.

TECHNOLOGY

Go to the Glencoe Science Web site at **science.glencoe.com** or use the **Glencoe Science CD-ROM** for additional chapter assessment.

THE PRINCETON REVIEW   Test Practice

Magnetism affects all aspects of modern life. The table below lists some examples of processes involving magnetic fields.

Processes Involving Magnetic Fields		
Example	**Process**	**Result**
Motor	Converts electrical energy into kinetic	Used in elecric fans
Generator	Converts mechanical energy into electrical	Produce light
Charged particles from Sun	Charged particles trapped in Earth's magnetosphere	Aurora
Transformer	Change voltage through power lines	Deliver current to homes

Study the table and answer the following questions.

1. According to this information, which process most likely occurs naturally?
   A) conversion of electrical energy into kinetic
   B) conversion of mechanical energy into electric energy
   C) trapped charged particles in Earth's magnetosphere
   D) voltage changes through power lines

2. Hydroelectric power plants use the gravitational potential energy of water to turn generators, which then produce electricity. According to the table above, which process is this an example of?
   F) motor   H) charged particles
   G) generator   J) transformer

Electronics and Computers

Electronic components like these are used in televisions, CD players, and computers. Some of these components can be made so small that some electronic devices, such as computers, can contain millions of them. In this chapter you will learn what electronic components do. You also will learn how computers use these components to store and process information.

What do you think?

Science Journal Look at the picture below with a classmate. Discuss what you think this might be or what is happening. Here's a hint: *You'll find these in almost any computer.* Write down your answer or best guess in your Science Journal.

Imagine how your life would be different if you had been born before the invention of electronic devices. You could not watch television or listen to music on a tape or CD player. You would have no computer to use to write and spell check your papers, look up information on the Internet, or play games. See for yourself how electronic devices can make some tasks easier during this activity.

Compare calculators

1. Use a stopwatch to time how long it takes a volunteer to add the numbers 423, 21, 84, and 1,098.

2. Time how long it takes another volunteer to add these numbers using a calculator.

3. Repeat steps 1 and 2 but ask the competitors to multiply 149 and 876.

4. Divide the time needed by the student calculator by the time needed by the calculator to solve each problem. How many times faster is the calculator?

Observe

Write a paragraph in your Science Journal describing which step in each calculation takes the most time for the student and for the electronic calculator.

Before You Read

Making a Know-Want-Learn Study Fold Make the following Foldable to help identify what you already know and what you want to know about electronics.

1. Place a sheet of paper in front of you so the long side is at the top. Fold the paper in half from top to bottom.

2. Fold in the left side and the right side. Unfold the paper so three sections show.

3. Through the top thickness of paper, cut along each of the fold lines to the topfold, forming three tabs. Label the tabs *Know, Want,* and *Learned.*

4. Before you read the chapter, write what you know under the left tab and what you want to know under the middle tab. As you read the chapter, add to and correct what you have written.

Electronics

Electronic Signals

You've popped some popcorn, put a video in the VCR, and turned off the lights. Now you're ready to watch a movie. The VCR, television, and lamp shown in **Figure 1** use electricity to operate. However, unlike the lamp, the VCR and the TV are electronic devices. An electronic device uses electricity to store, process, and transfer information.

The VCR and the TV use information recorded on the video tape to produce the images and sounds you see as a movie. As the video tape moves inside the VCR, it produces a changing electric current. This changing electric current is the information the VCR uses to send signals to the TV. The TV then uses these signals to produce the images you see and the sounds you hear.

A changing electric current that carries information is an **electronic signal.** The information can be used to produce sounds, images, printed words, numbers, or other data. For example, a changing electric current causes a loudspeaker to produce sound. If the electric current didn't change, no sound would be produced by the loudspeaker. There are two types of electronic signals—analog and digital.

Analog Signals Most TVs, VCRs, radios and telephones process and transmit information that is in the form of analog electronic signals. An analog signal is a signal that varies smoothly in time. In an analog electronic signal the electric current increases or decreases smoothly in time, just as your hand can move smoothly up and down.

Electronic signals are not the only types of analog signals. An analog signal can be produced by something that varies in a smooth, continuous way and contains information. For example, a person's temperature changes smoothly and contains information about a person's health.

Figure 1
The information contained on a video tape is converted to electronic signals by the VCR. The VCR sends these signals to the TV, which uses the information to produce images and sound.

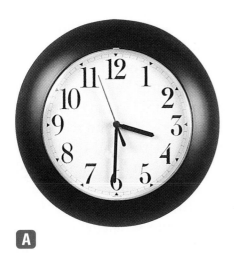

Figure 2
Clocks can be analog or digital devices. **A** The information displayed on an analog device such as this clock changes continuously. **B** On this digital clock, the displayed time jumps from one number to another.

Analog Devices The clock with hands shown in **Figure 2A** is an example of an analog device. The hands move smoothly from one number to the next to represent the time of day. Fluid-filled and dial thermometers also are analog devices. In a fluid-filled thermometer, the height of the fluid column smoothly rises or falls as the temperature changes. In a dial thermometer, a spring smoothly expands or contracts as the temperature changes.

You have used another analog device if you ever have made a recording on a magnetic tape player. When voices or music are recorded on magnetic tape, the tape stores an analog signal of the sounds. When you play the tape, the tape player converts the analog signal to an electric current. This current changes smoothly with time and causes a loudspeaker to vibrate, re-creating the sounds for you to hear.

Digital Signals Some devices, such as CD players, use a different kind of electronic signal called a digital signal. Unlike an analog signal, a **digital signal** does not vary smoothly, but changes in jumps or steps. If each jump is represented by a number, a digital signal can be represented by a series of numbers.

✔ **Reading Check** *How is a digital signal different from an analog signal?*

You might have a digital clock or watch similar to the one shown in **Figure 2B** that displays the time as numbers. The display changes from 6:29 to 6:30 in a single jump, rather than sweeping smoothly from second to second. You might have seen digital thermometers that display temperature as a number. Some digital thermometers display temperature to the nearest degree, such as 23°C. The displayed temperature changes by jumps of 1°C. As a result, temperatures between two whole degrees, such as 22.7°C, are not displayed.

Digitized Analog Signal

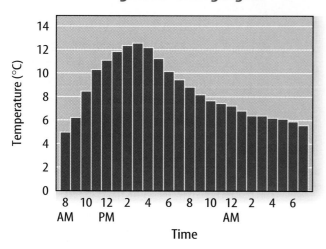

Making Digital Signals A smoothly varying analog signal can be converted to a digital signal. For example, suppose you wish to create a record of how the temperature outside changed over a day. One way to do this would be read an outdoor thermometer every hour and record the temperature and time. At the end of the day your temperature record would be a series of numbers. If you used these numbers to make a graph of the temperature record, it might look like the one shown in **Figure 3.** The temperature information shown by the graph changes in steps and is a digital signal.

Figure 3
A temperature record made by recording the temperature every hour changes in steps and is a digital signal.

Figure 4
An analog signal can be converted to a digital signal. At a fixed time interval, the strength of the analog signal is measured and recorded. The resulting digital signal changes in steps.

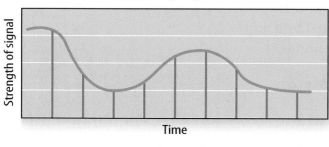

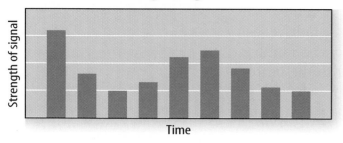

Sampling an Analog Signal By recording the temperature every hour, you have sampled the smoothly varying outdoor temperature. When an analog signal is sampled, a value of the signal is read and recorded at some time interval, such as every hour or every second. An example is shown in **Figure 4.** As a result, a smoothly changing analog signal is converted to a series of numbers. This series of numbers is a digital signal.

The process of converting an analog signal to a digital signal is called digitization. The analog signal on a magnetic tape can be converted to a digital signal by sampling. In this way, a song can be represented by a series of numbers.

Using Digital Signals It might seem that analog signals would be more useful than digital signals. After all, when an analog signal is converted to a digital signal, some information is lost. However, think about how analog and digital signals might be stored. Suppose a song that is stored as an analog signal on a small cassette tape were digitized and converted into a series of numbers. It might take millions of numbers to digitize a song, so how could these numbers be stored? As you will see later in this chapter, there is one electronic device that can store these numbers easily—a computer.

Once a digital signal is stored on a computer as a series of numbers, the computer can change these numbers using mathematical formulas. This process changes the signal and is called signal processing. For example, background noise can be removed from a digitized song using signal processing.

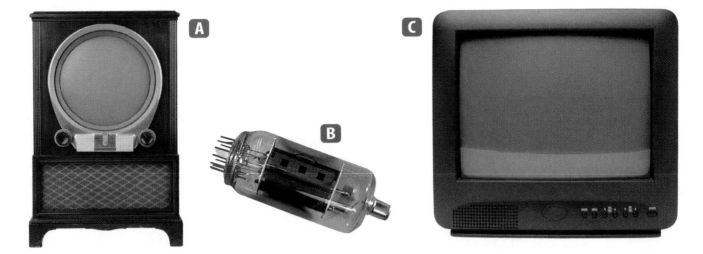

Electronic Devices

An electronic device, such as a calculator or a CD player, uses the information contained in electronic signals to do a job. For example, the job can be adding two numbers together or making sounds and images. The electronic signals are electric currents that flow through circuits in the electronic device. An electronic device, such as a calculator or a VCR, may contain hundreds or thousands of complex electric circuits.

Electronic Components The electric circuits in an electronic device usually contain electronic components. These electronic components are small devices that use the information in the electronic signals to control the flow of current in the circuits.

Early electronic devices, such as the television shown in **Figure 5A,** used electronic components called vacuum tubes, such as the one shown in **Figure 5B,** to help create sounds and images. Vacuum tubes were bulky and generated a great deal of heat. As a result, early electronic devices used more electrical power and were less dependable than those used today, such as the television shown in **Figure 5C.** Today, televisions and radios no longer use vacuum tubes. Instead, they contain electronic components made from semiconductors.

Semiconductors

On the periodic table, the small number of elements found between the metals and nonmetals are called metalloids. Some metalloids, such as silicon and germanium, are semiconductors. A **semiconductor** is an element that is a poorer conductor of electricity than metals but a better conductor than nonmetals. However, semiconductors have a special property that ordinary conductors and insulators lack—their electrical conductivity can be controlled by adding impurities.

Figure 5
Because early televisions and radios used vacuum tubes, they were bigger, heavier, and less reliable than their modern versions.

Research Visit the Glencoe Science Web site at **science.glenoce.com** for more information about semiconductor devices. Choose an application of one device and prepare a brief presentation about it.

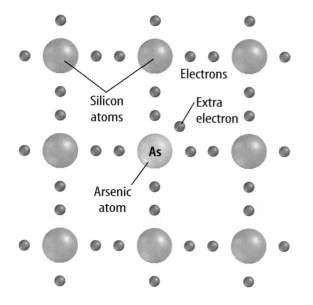

Figure 6
When arsenic atoms are added to a silicon crystal, they produce extra electrons that are free to move about. This causes the electrical conductivity of the silicon crystal to increase.

Figure 7
Diodes like these are wired into electronic circuits to help control the flow of electric current. Diodes allow current to flow in only one direction.

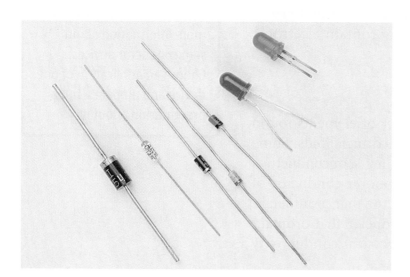

Adding Impurities Adding even a single atom of an element such as gallium or arsenic to a million silicon atoms significantly changes the conductivity. This process of adding impurities is called doping.

Doping can produce two different kinds of semiconductors. One type of semiconductor can be created by adding atoms like arsenic to a silicon crystal, as shown in **Figure 6.** Then the silicon crystal contains extra electrons. A semiconductor with extra electrons is an n-type semiconductor.

A p-type semiconductor is produced when atoms like gallium are added to a silicon crystal. Then the silicon crystal has fewer electrons than it had before. An n-type semiconductor can give, or donate, electrons and a p-type semiconductor can take, or accept, electrons.

Solid-State Components

The two types of semiconductors can be put together to form electronic components that can control the flow of electric current in a circuit. Combinations of n-type and p-type semiconductors can form components that behave like switches that can be turned off and on. Other combinations can form components that can increase, or amplify, the change in an electric current or voltage. Electronic components that are made from combinations of semiconductors are called solid-state components. Diodes and transistors are examples of solid-state components that often are used in electric circuits.

Diodes A **diode** is a solid-state component that, like a one-way street, allows current to flow only in one direction. In a diode, a p-type semiconductor is connected to an n-type semiconductor. Because an n-type semiconductor gives electrons and a p-type semiconductor accepts electrons, current can flow from the n-type to the p-type semiconductor, but not in the opposite direction. **Figure 7** shows common types of diodes. Diodes are useful for converting alternating current (AC) to direct current (DC). Recall that an alternating current constantly changes direction. When an alternating current reaches a diode, the diode allows only the current in one direction through. The result is direct current.

Transistors A **transistor** is a solid-state component that can be used to amplify signals in an electric circuit. A transistor also is used as an electronic switch. Electronic signals can cause a transistor to allow current to pass through it or to block the flow of current. **Figure 8** shows examples of transistors that are used in many electronic devices. Unlike a diode, a transistor contains three layers of semiconductors joined together. An n-p-n transistor has a layer of p-type semiconductor sandwiched between two n-type semiconductors. A p-n-p transistor has a layer of n-type semiconductor sandwiched between two p-type semiconductors.

Figure 8
Transistors such as these are used in electric circuits to amplify signals or to act as switches.

 **Reading Check** *What are two ways that transistors are used in electronic circuits?*

Integrated Circuits The transistors you might see in an electronics store are about the size of a pencil eraser. Personal computers usually contain millions of transistors, and would be many times larger if they used transistors the size of pencil erasers. Instead, computers and other electronic devices use integrated circuits. An **integrated circuit** contains large numbers of interconnected solid-state components and is made from a single chip of semiconductor material such as silicon. An integrated circuit, like the one shown in **Figure 9,** may be smaller than 1 mm on each side and still can contain millions of transistors, diodes, and other components.

Figure 9
This tiny integrated circuit consists of thousands of diodes and transistors, yet is smaller than your fingertip.

Section ① Assessment

1. How are analog signals different from digital signals?
2. Why are semiconductors useful in electronic devices?
3. How are diodes and transistors used?
4. Explain the difference between p-type semiconductors and n-type semiconductors.
5. **Think Critically** In sampling an analog signal, what are the advantages and disadvantages of decreasing the time interval?

Skill Builder Activities

6. **Researching Information** Use references to find several ways that integrated circuits are used. Write a paragraph that summarizes your findings. **For more help, refer to the** Science Skill Handbook.
7. **Concept Mapping** Use a concept map to show the relationship between electronic signals, circuits, components, and devices. **For more help, refer to the** Science Skill Handbook.

Activity

Investigating Diodes

Diodes are found in most electronic devices. They are used to control the flow of electrons through a circuit. Electrons will flow through a diode in only one direction, from the n-type semiconductor to the p-type semiconductor. In this activity you will use a type of diode called an LED (light-emitting diode) to observe how a diode works.

What You'll Investigate
How does a current flow through a diode?

Materials
light-emitting diode
lightbulb and holder
D-cell battery and holder
wire

Goals
■ **Create** an electronic circuit.
■ **Observe** how an LED works.

3. Reverse the connections on the LED so the current goes into the opposite end. Observe whether the LED lights up this time. Record your observation.

Procedure

1. Set up the circuit shown below. Record your observations. Then reverse the connections so each wire is connected to the other battery terminals. Record your observations.

2. Disconnect the wires from the lightbulb and attach one wire to each end of an LED. Observe whether the LED lights up when you connect the battery.

Conclude and Apply

1. **Explain** why the bulb did or did not light up.

2. **Explain** why the LED did or did not light up each time.

3. How is the behavior of the lightbulb different from that of the LED?

4. Based on your observations, infer which wire on the LED is connected to the n-type semiconductor and which is connected to the p-type semiconductor.

1.5V Battery

Lightbulb

Communicating **Your Data**

Discuss your results with other students in your class. Did their LEDs behave in the same way? **For more help, refer to the** Science Skill Handbook.

2 Computers

What are computers?

When was the last time you used a computer? Computers are found in libraries, grocery stores, banks, and gas stations. Computers seem to be everywhere. A computer is an electronic device that can carry out a set of instructions, or a program. By changing the program, the same computer can be made to do a different job.

Compared to today's desktop and laptop computers, the first electronic computers, like the one shown in **Figure 10A,** were much bigger and slower. Several of the first electronic computers were built in the United States between 1946 and 1951. Solid-state components and the integrated circuit had not been developed yet. So these early computers contained thousands of vacuum tubes that used a great deal of electric power and produced large amounts of heat.

Computers became much smaller, faster, and more efficient after integrated circuits became available in the 1960s. Today, even a game system, like the one in **Figure 10B,** can carry out many more operations each second than the early computers.

As You Read

What You'll Learn
- **Describe** the different parts of a computer.
- **Compare** computer hardware with computer software.
- **Discuss** the different types of memory and storage in a computer.

Vocabulary
binary system
random-access memory
read-only memory
computer software
microprocessor

Why It's Important
You can use computers for a variety of applications if you understand how they work.

A

Figure 10
A One of the first electronic computers was ENIAC, which was developed by the U.S. Army in 1946 and weighed more than 30 tons. ENIAC could do 5,000 additions per second. **B** This modern game system can do millions of operations per second.

B

Using Binary Numbers

Procedure

1. Cut out **8 small paper squares.**
2. On four of the squares, draw the number zero, and on the other four, draw the number one.
3. Use the numbered squares to help determine the number of different combinations possible from four binary digits. List the combinations.

Analysis

1. From **Table 1** and your results from this MiniLAB, what happens to the number of combinations each time the number of binary digits is increased by one?
2. Infer how many combinations would be possible using five binary digits.

Table 1 Combinations of Binary Digits	
Number of Binary Digits	**Possible Combinations**
1	0 1
2	00 01 10 11
3	000 001 010 011 100 101 110 111

Computer Information

How does a computer display images, generate sounds, and manipulate numbers and words? Every piece of information that is stored in or used by a computer must be converted to a series of numbers. The words you write with a word processor, or the numbers in a spreadsheet are stored in the computer's memory as numbers. An image or a sound file also is stored as a series of numbers. Information stored in this way is sometimes called digital information.

Binary Numbers Imagine what it would be like if you had to communicate with just two words—on and off. Could you use these words to describe your favorite music or to read a book out loud? Communication with just two words seems impossible, but that's exactly what a computer does.

All the digital information in a computer is converted to a type of number that is expressed using only two digits—0 and 1. This type of number is called a binary (BI nuh ree) number. Each 0 or 1 is called a binary digit, or bit. Because this number system uses only two digits, it is called the **binary system,** or base-2 number system.

✔ **Reading Check** *Which digits are used in the binary system?*

Combining Binary Digits You might think that using only two digits would limit the amount of information you can represent. However, a small number of binary digits can be used to generate a large number of combinations, as shown in **Table 1.**

While one binary digit has only two possible combinations—0 or 1—there are four possible combinations for a group of two binary digits, as shown in **Table 1.** By using just one more binary digit the possible number of combinations is increased to eight. The number of combinations increases quickly as more binary digits are added to the group. For example, there are 65,536 combinations possible for a group of sixteen binary digits.

Representing Information with Binary Digits Combinations of binary digits can be used to represent information. For example, the English alphabet has 26 letters. Suppose each letter was represented by one combination of binary digits. To represent both lower case and upper case letters would require a total of 52 different combinations of binary digits. Would a group of five binary digits have enough possible combinations?

Representing Letters and Numbers A common system that is used by computers represents each letter, number, or other text character by eight binary digits, or one byte. There are 256 combinations possible for a group of eight binary digits. In this system, the letter "A" is represented by the byte 01000001, while the letter "a" is represented by the byte 01100001, and a question mark is represented by 00111111.

Computer memory

Why are digital signals stored in a computer as binary numbers? A binary number is a series of bits that can have only one of two values—0 and 1. A switch, such as a light switch on a wall, can have two positions: on or off. A switch could be used to represent the two values of a bit. A switch in the "off" position could represent a 0, and a switch in the "on" position could represent a 1. **Table 2** shows how switches could be used to represent combinations of binary digits.

Table 2 Representing Binary Digits

Binary Number	Switches
0000	
0001	
0010	
0011	
0100	
1010	

Problem-Solving Activity

How much information can be stored?

Information can be stored in a computer's memory or in storage devices such as hard disks or CDs. One letter, number, or other text character can be represented by one byte of information. The amount of information that can be stored in a computer's memory or on a hard disk is so large that special units are used. The table shows some of the units that are used to describe amounts of information. Desktop computers often have hard disks that can store many gigabytes of information. How much information can be stored in one gigabyte of storage?

Identifying the Problem

When words are stored on a computer, every letter, punctuation mark, and space between words is represented by one byte. A page of text, such as this page, might contain as many as 2,900 characters. So to store a page of text on a computer might require 2,900 bytes.

Size of Information Storage Units

Information Storage Unit	Number of Bytes
kilobyte	1,024
megabyte	1,048,576
gigabyte	1,073,741,824

If you write a page of text using a word-processing program, more bytes might be needed to store the page. This is because when the page is stored, some word-processing programs include other information along with the text.

Solving the Problem

1. If it takes 2,900 bytes to store one page of text on a computer, how many pages can be stored in 1 gigabyte of storage?
2. Suppose a book contains 400 pages of text. How many books could be stored on a 1-gigabyte hard disk?
3. A CD can hold 650 megabytes of information. How many 400-page books could be stored on a CD?

Figure 11
Computer memory is made of integrated circuits like this one. This integrated circuit can contain millions of microscopic circuits, shown here under high magnification.

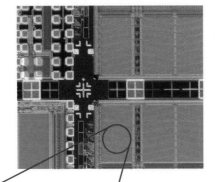

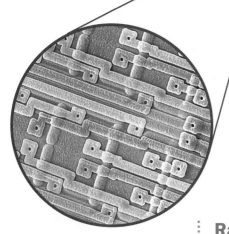

Research Visit the Glencoe Science Web site at **science.glencoe.com** for more information about types of computer programs. Choose an application of one program and explain why it is useful. Create a simple chart summarizing what the program does.

Storing Information The memory in a computer is an integrated circuit that contains millions of tiny electronic circuits, as shown in **Figure 11.** In the most commonly used type of computer memory, each circuit is able to store electric charge and can be either charged or uncharged. If the circuit is charged, it represents the bit 1 and if it is uncharged it represents the bit 0. Because computer memory contains millions of these circuits, it can store tremendous amounts of information using only the numbers 1 and 0.

What is your earliest memory? When you remember something from long ago, you use your long-term memory. On the other hand, when you work on a math problem, you may keep the numbers in your head long enough to find the answer. Like you, a computer has a long-term memory and a temporary memory that are used for different purposes.

Random-Access Memory A computer's **random-access memory,** or RAM, is temporary memory that stores documents, programs, and data while they are being used. Program instructions and data are temporarily stored in RAM while you are using a program or changing the data.

For example, a computer game is kept in RAM while you are playing it. If you are using a word-processing program to write a report, the report is temporarily held in RAM while you are working on it. Because information stored in RAM is lost when the computer is turned off, this type of memory cannot store anything that you want to use later.

The amount of RAM depends on the number of binary digits it can store. Recall that eight bits is called a byte. A megabyte is more than one million bytes. A computer that has 128 megabytes of memory can store more than 128 million bytes of information in its RAM, or nearly one billion bits.

 **Reading Check** *What happens to information in RAM when the computer is turned off?*

Read-Only Memory Some information that is needed to enable the computer to operate is stored in its permanent memory. The computer can read this memory, but it cannot be changed. Memory that can't be changed and is permanently stored inside the computer is called **read-only memory** or ROM. ROM is not lost when the computer is turned off.

Computer Programs

It's your mother's birthday and you decide to surprise her by baking a chocolate cake. You find a recipe for chocolate cake in a cookbook and follow the directions in the order the recipe tells you to. However, if the person who wrote the recipe left out any steps or put them in the wrong order, the cake probably will not turn out the way you expected. A computer program is like a recipe. A program is a series of instructions that tell the computer how to do a job. Unlike the recipe for a cake, some computer programs contain millions of instructions that tell the computer how to do many different jobs.

All the functions of a computer, such as displaying an image on the computer monitor or doing a math calculation, are controlled by programs. These instructions tell the computer how to add two numbers, how to display a word, or how to change an image on the monitor when you move a joystick. Many different programs can be stored in a computer's memory.

Computer Software When you type a report, play a video game, draw a picture, or look through an encyclopedia on a computer, you are using computer software. **Computer software** is any list of instructions for the computer. The instructions that are part of the software tell the computer what to display on the monitor. If you respond to what you see, for example by moving the mouse, the software instructions tell the computer how to respond to your action.

Computer Programming

The process of writing computer software is called computer programming. To write a computer program, you must decide what you want the computer to do, plan the best way to organize the instructions, write the instructions, and test the program to be sure it works. A person who writes computer programs is called a computer programmer. Computer programmers write software in computer languages such as Basic, C++, and Java. **Figure 12** shows part of a computer program. After the program is written, it is converted into binary digits in order to be stored in the computer's memory. Then the computer can carry out the program's instructions.

Mini LAB

Observing Memory
Procedure
1. Write a different five-digit number on six **3 × 5 cards.**
2. Show a card to a partner for 3 s. Turn the card over and ask your partner to repeat the number. Repeat with two other cards.
3. Repeat this procedure with the last three cards, but wait 20 s before asking your partner to repeat each number.

Analysis
1. Is your partner's memory of the five-digit numbers more like computer RAM or ROM? Explain.

Figure 12
This is part of a computer program that directs the operation of a computer.

```
int request_dma(unsigned int dmanr, const char * device_id)
{
    if (dmanr > = MAX_DMA_CHANNELS)
        return -EINVAL;

    if (xchg(&dma_chan_busy[dmanr].lock, 1) != 0)
        return -EBUSY;

    dma_chan_busy[dmanr].device_id = device_id;

    /* old flag was 0, now contains 1 to indicate busy */
    return 0;
} /* request_dma */

void free_dma(unsigned int dmanr)
{
    if (dmanr > = MAX_DMA_CHANNELS) {
        printk("Trying to free DMA%d\n", dmanr);
        return;
    }
}
```

Computer Hardware

When you press a key on a computer's keyboard, a letter appears on the screen. This seems to occur all at once, but actually three steps are involved. In the first step, the computer receives information from an input device, such as a keyboard or mouse. For example, when you press a key on the keyboard, the computer receives and stores an electronic signal from the keyboard.

The next step is to process the input signal from the keyboard. This means to change the input signal into an electronic signal that can be understood by the computer monitor. The computer does this by following instructions contained in the programs stored in the computer's memory. The third step is to send the processed signal to the monitor.

All three steps can be carried out with a combination of hardware and software components. Computer hardware consists of input devices, output devices, storage devices, and integrated circuits for storing information. A keyboard and a mouse are examples of input devices, while a monitor, a printer, and loudspeakers are examples of output devices. Storage devices, such as floppy disks, hard disks, and CDs, are used to store information outside of the computer memory. A computer also contains a microprocessor that controls the computer hardware. Examples of computer hardware are shown in **Figure 13.**

Figure 13
Computer hardware includes input devices, output devices, and storage devices.

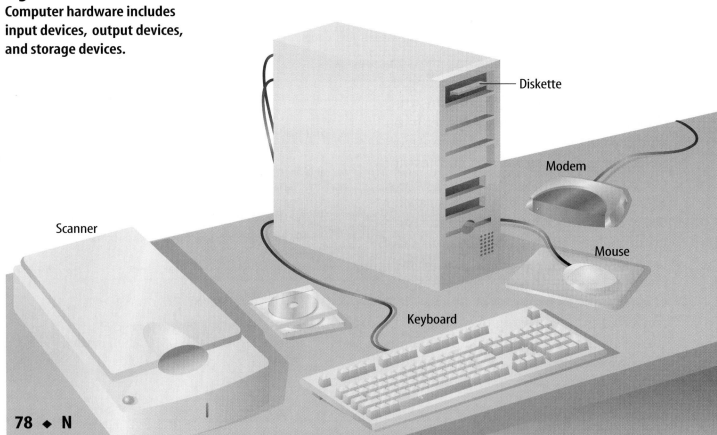

The Microprocessor Modern computers contain a microprocessor, like the one shown in **Figure 14,** that serves as the brain of the computer. A **microprocessor,** which is also called the central processing unit, or CPU, is an integrated circuit that controls the flow of information between different parts of the computer. A microprocessor can contain millions of interconnected transistors and other components. The microprocessor receives electronic signals from various parts of the computer, processes these signals, and sends electronic signals to other parts of the computer. For example, the microprocessor might tell the hard-disk drive to write data to the hard disk or the monitor to change the image on the screen. The microprocessor does this by carrying out instructions that are contained in computer programs stored in the computer's memory.

The microprocessor was developed in the late 1970s as the result of a process that made it possible to fit thousands of electronic components on a silicon chip. In the 1980s, the number of components on a silicon chip increased to hundreds of thousands. In the 1990s, microprocessors were developed that contained several million components on a single chip.

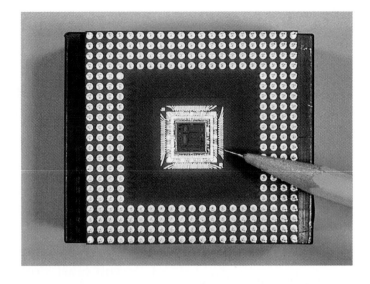

Figure 14
A microprocessor is an integrated circuit that carries out the instructions contained in computer programs. It can contain millions of transistors and other solid-state components.

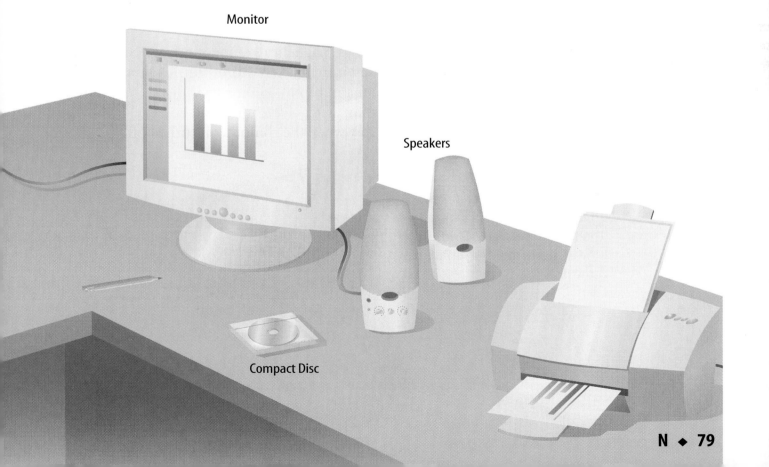

Monitor

Speakers

Compact Disc

Storing Information

You have decided to type your homework assignment on a computer. The resulting paper is quite long and you make many changes to it each time you read it. How does the computer make it possible for you to store your information and make changes to it?

Both RAM and ROM are integrated circuits inside the computer. You might wonder, then, why other types of information storage are needed. Information stored in RAM is lost when the computer is turned off, and information stored in ROM can only be read—it can't be changed. If you want to store information that can be changed but isn't lost when the computer is off, you must store that information on a storage device, such as a disk. Several different types of disks are available.

Hard Disks A hard disk is a device that stores computer information magnetically. A hard disk is usually located inside a computer. **Figure 15** shows the inside of a hard disk, and **Figure 16** shows how a hard disk stores data. The hard disk contains one or more metal disks that have magnetic particles on one surface. When you save information on a hard disk, a device called a read/write head inside the disk drive changes the orientation of the magnetic particles on the disk's surface. Orientation in one direction represents 0 and orientation in the opposite direction represents 1. When a magnetized disk is read, the read/write head converts the digital information on the disk to pulses of electric current.

Information stored magnetically cannot be read by the computer as quickly as information stored on RAM and ROM. However, because the information on a hard disk is stored magnetically rather than with electronic switches like RAM, the information isn't lost when the computer is turned off.

Figure 15
A hard disk contains a disk or platter that is coated with magnetic particles. A read/write head moves over the surface of the disk.

Figure 16

Computers are useful because they can process large amounts of information quickly. Almost all desktop computers use a hard disk to store information. A hard disk is an electronic filing cabinet that can store enormous amounts of information and retrieve them quickly.

Read/Write head

Platters

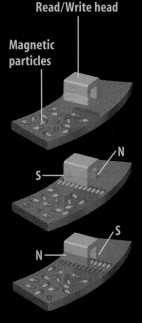

Read/Write head

Magnetic particles

B To write information on the disk, a magnetic field is created around the head by an electric current. As the platter rotates past the head, this magnetic field causes the magnetic particles on the platter to line up in bands. One direction of the bands corresponds to the digital bit 0, the other to the digital bit 1.

A A hard-disk drive is made of a stack of aluminum disks, called platters, that are coated with a thin layer that contains magnetic particles. Like tiny compasses, these particles will line up along magnetic field lines. The hard disk also contains read/write heads that contain electromagnets. When the hard disk is turned on, the platters spin under the heads.

C To read information on the disk, no current is sent to the heads. Instead, the magnetized bands create a changing current in the head as it passes over the platter. This current is the electronic signal that represents the needed information.

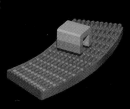

Figure 17
An optical storage disk stores information that is read by a laser. **A** Information is stored on an optical disk by a series of pits and flat spots, representing a binary 1 or 0. **B** CDs, laser disks, and DVDs are all examples of optical storage disks.

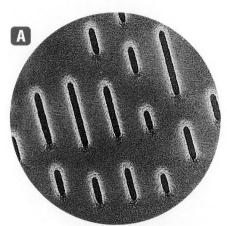

Floppy Disks Storing information on a hard disk is convenient, but sometimes you might want to store information that you can carry with you. The original storage device of this type was the floppy disk. A floppy disk is a thin, flexible, plastic disk. You might be confused by the term *floppy* if you have heard it used to describe disks that seem quite rigid. That is because you don't actually hold the floppy disk. Instead, you hold the harder plastic case in which the floppy disk is encased. Just as for a hard disk, the floppy disk is coated with a magnetic material that is magnetized and read by a read/write head. Floppy disks have lower storage capacity than hard disks. Also, compared to hard disks, information is read from and written to floppy disks much more slowly.

Optical Disks An optical storage disk, such as a CD, is a thin, plastic disk that has information digitally stored on it. The disk contains a series of microscopic pits and flat spots as shown in **Figure 17A.** A tiny laser beam shines on the surface of the disk. The information on the disk is read by measuring the intensity of the laser light reflected from the surface of the disk. This intensity will depend on whether the laser beam strikes a pit or a flat spot. The original optical storage disks, laser discs, CD-ROMs, and DVD-ROMs, were read-only. Several of these are shown in **Figure 17B.** However, CD-RW disks can be erased and rewritten many times. Information is written by a CD burner that causes a metal alloy in the disk to change form when heated by a laser. When the disk is read, the intensity of reflected laser light depends on which form of the alloy the beam strikes.

Computer Networks

Your class is about to start a new project. You will communicate with a class in a school in another state using a computer. People can communicate using a computer if it is part of a computer network. A computer network is two or more computers that are connected to share files or other information. The computers might be linked by cables, telephone lines, or radio signals.

The Internet is a collection of linked computer networks from all over the world. For example, a university in one city might have all of its computers networked. A large company with offices in several cities can do the same. The Internet is thousands of these smaller networks linked together by cable or satellite. The Internet itself has no information. No documents or files exist on the Internet, but you can use the Internet to access a tremendous amount of information by linking to other computers.

The World Wide Web is part of the Internet. The World Wide Web is the ever-changing collection of information (text, graphics, audio, and video) on computers all over the world. The computers that store these documents are called servers. When you connect with a server through the Internet, you can view any of the Web documents that are stored there, like the web page shown in **Figure 18.** A particular collection of information that is stored in one place is known as a Web site.

Figure 18
When you connect to the Internet, you can be linked with other computers that are part of the World Wide Web. Then you can have access to the information stored at millions of Web sites.

Section 2 Assessment

1. What is the binary system and why is it useful for storing information?

2. What are RAM and ROM?

3. How is computer software different from computer hardware?

4. List and describe at least three different types of information storage devices.

5. **Think Critically** How is the World Wide Web related to the Internet? How can the Internet and the World Wide Web change the way in which a business operates?

Skill Builder Activities

6. **Comparing and Contrasting** Compare and contrast floppy disks, optical disks, and hard disks. **For more help, refer to the** Science Skill Handbook.

7. **Concept Mapping** Develop a spider map with "Computers" in the center box. Include the following terms: keyboard, monitor, microprocessor, programs, RAM, ROM, floppy disk, hard disk, CD, and Internet. **For more help, refer to the** Science Skill Handbook.

Does your computer have a virus?

The Internet has provided many ways to share information and become connected with people near and far. People can communicate ideas and information quickly and easily. Unfortunately, some people use computers and the Internet as an opportunity to create and spread computer viruses. Many new viruses are created each year that can damage information and programs on a computer. Viruses create problems for computers in homes and schools. Computer problems caused by viruses can be costly for business and government computers, as well. Find out what you can do to protect your computer from viruses.

Recognize the Problem

How can acquiring and transmitting computer viruses be prevented?

Form a Hypothesis

People share information and ideas by exchanging electronic files with one other. Perhaps you send email to your friends and family. Many people send word processing or spreadsheet files to friends and associates. What happens if a computer file is infected with a virus? How is that virus spread among different users? How can you protect your computer and your information from being attacked by a virus?

Goals
- **Understand** what a computer virus is.
- **Identify** different types of computer viruses.
- **Describe** how a computer virus is spread.
- **Create** a plan for protecting electronic files and computers from computer viruses.

Data Source

SCIENCE *Online* Go to the Glencoe Science Web site at **science.glencoe.com** to get more information about computer viruses and for data collected by other students.

Test Your Hypothesis

Plan

1. Do research to find out what a computer virus is and the difference between various types of viruses. Also research the ways that a computer virus can damage computer files and programs.

2. After you know what a computer virus is, make a list of different types of viruses and how they are passed from computer to computer. For example, some viruses can be passed through attachments to email. Others can be passed by sharing spreadsheet files. Be specific about how a virus is passed.

3. Discover how you can protect yourself from viruses that attack your computer. Make a list of steps to follow to avoid infection.

Do

1. Make sure your teacher approves your plan before you start.

2. Go to the Glencoe Science Web site at **science.glencoe.com** to post your data.

Analyze Your Data

1. How are computer viruses transferred from one computer to another?

2. How can you prevent your computer from becoming infected by a virus?

3. How can you prevent other people from getting computer viruses?

What steps should you take to make sure you do not spread viruses to people you share information with?

4. Describe the different ways computer viruses can damage computer files and programs.

Draw Conclusions

1. **Create** a list of five to eight steps a computer user should follow to prevent getting a computer virus or passing a virus to someone else.

2. Discuss how anti-virus software can keep viruses from spreading. Could anti-virus software always prevent you from getting a computer virus? Why or why not?

*C*ommunicating
Your Data

SCIENCE *Online* Find this *Use the Internet* activity on the Glencoe Science Web site at **science.glencoe.com.** Post your data in the table that is provided. **Compare** your data on types of viruses and how they infect computers with that of other students.

E-Lectrifying

Here's a look at how computers and the Internet are changing what—and how—you read

E-Books

In recent years, people have been using their computers to order books from online bookstores. That's no big deal. What might become a big deal is the ordering of electronic books—books that you download to your own computer and read on the screen or print out to read later. Some famous authors are writing books just for that purpose. Some of the books are published only online—you can't find them anywhere else.

Many other Web sites, however, are selling any book anybody wishes to write—including students like you. In fact, you could start your own online bookstore with your own stories and reports. This is a big change from the recent past, when publishers controlled what got published. Now you can have that control.

It will be up to readers to pick and choose what's good from the huge number of e-books that will be on the Web.

Curling Up with a Good Disk

Downloading books to your home computer is just one way to get an e-book. You can also buy versions of books to read on hand-held devices that are about the size of a paperback book. With one device, the books come on CD-ROM disks. With another, the books download to the device over a modem.

The e-book devices currently are expensive, heavy, and awkward and the number of books you can get for them is small. But if improvements come quickly, it might not be long before you check out of the library with a pocketful of disks instead of a heavy armload of books!

Will Traditional Books Disappear?

Most people think that the traditional printed book will never disappear. Publishers will still be printing books on paper with soft and hard covers. But publishers also predict there will be more and more kinds of formats for books. E-books, for example, might be best for interactive works that blend video, sound, and words the way many Web sites already do. For example, an e-book biography might allow the reader to click on photos and videos of the subject, and even provide links to other sources of information. Still, as writer Anne Glusker says, "There will be times when nothing but the feel, smell, and look of a beautifully printed and bound book will satisfy."

All of these stacked books can fit into one e-book.

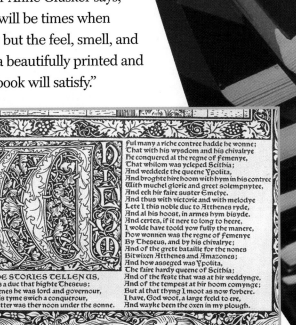

E-books have come a long way since this early printed book.

CONNECTIONS Interview Talk to a bookstore employee to find out how book publishing and selling has changed in the last five years. Can he or she predict how people will read books in the future? Report to the class. Then brainstorm how writing you've done could be uploaded to a Web site.

SCIENCE *Online*

For more information, visit science.glencoe.com.

Reviewing Main Ideas

Section 1 Electronics

1. A changing electric current used to carry information is an electronic signal. Electronic signals can be either analog or digital. *Which of these disks contains digital information?*

2. Semiconductor elements, such as silicon and germanium, conduct electricity better than nonmetals but not as well as metals. If a small amount of some impurities is added to a semiconductor, its conductivity can be controlled.

3. Diodes and transistors are solid-state components. Diodes allow current to flow in one direction only. Transistors are used as switches or amplifiers. *What are two ways in which the transistor shown below is different from a vacuum tube?*

Section 2 Computers

1. The binary system consists of two digits, 0 and 1. Switches within electronic devices such as computers can store information by turning on (1) and off (0).

2. Electronic memory within a computer can be random-access (RAM) or read-only (ROM).

3. Computer hardware consists of the physical parts of a computer. Computer software is a list of instructions for a computer.

4. A microprocessor is a complex, integrated circuit that stores information, makes computations, and directs the actions of the computer.

5. Floppy disks, hard disks, and optical disks are types of computer information storage devices. *How is information stored differently on DVDs, such as the one shown here, than on a hard disk?*

6. The Internet is a collection of linked computer networks from all over the world.

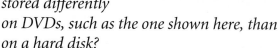

FOLDABLES
Reading & Study Skills

After You Read

Write what you learned under the tab of your Foldable. Using what you learned, explain why information is stored in computers as binary numbers.

Visualizing Main Ideas

Complete the following concept map on computers.

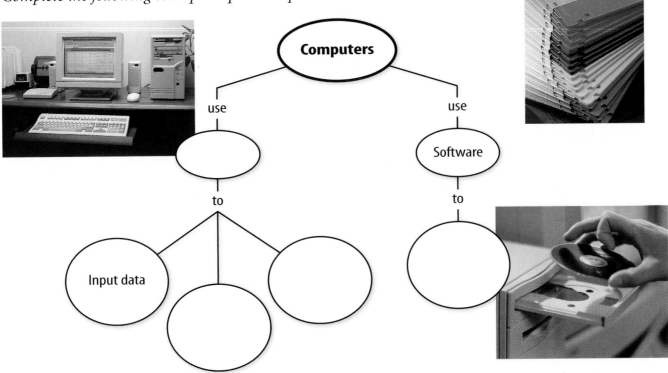

Vocabulary Review

Vocabulary Words

a. binary system
b. computer software
c. digital signal
d. diode
e. electronic signal
f. integrated circuit
g. microprocessor
h. random-access memory (RAM)
i. read-only memory (ROM)
j. semiconductor
k. transistor

THE PRINCETON REVIEW **Study Tip**

Sit with a study partner and read aloud to each other from a chapter. Then discuss what you've been reading with each other. Ask your teacher if you have any questions.

Using Vocabulary

Each of the following sentences is false. Make the sentence true by replacing the underlined word(s) with the correct vocabulary words.

1. RAM is a base-2 number system.

2. A transistor changes AC to DC.

3. An electronic signal contains thousands of electronic components.

4. A microprocessor is not a good conductor or insulator of current.

5. The information in ROM changes each time a computer is used.

6. A diode is an electronic device that can be used as a switch or to amplify signals.

7. A CPU is another name for a transistor.

Chapter 3 Assessment

Checking Concepts

Choose the word or phrase that best answers the question.

1. How is a digital signal different from an analog signal?
   A) It uses electric current.
   B) It changes continuously.
   C) It changes in steps.
   D) It is limited to computers.

2. What type of elements are semiconductors?
   A) metals
   B) nonmetals
   C) metalloids
   D) gases

3. Which type of semiconductor device can be used as an amplifier?
   A) diode
   B) transistor
   C) capacitor
   D) LED

4. Which type of electronic device is made up of one n-type and one p-type semiconductor joined together?
   A) capacitor
   B) transistor
   C) integrated circuit
   D) diode

5. What is the name of the number system used by computers for storing and transferring information?
   A) ROM
   B) decimal
   C) digital
   D) binary

6. Which type of computer memory is used by a computer to run a program?
   A) ROM
   B) RAM
   C) DVD
   D) hard disk

7. Which type of computer memory is used when the computer is first turned on?
   A) ROM
   B) RAM
   C) DVD
   D) hard disk

8. What part of a computer carries out the instructions contained in programs?
   A) RAM
   B) ROM
   C) LED
   D) microprocessor

9. Which of the following uses magnetic materials to store digital information?
   A) compact disk
   B) hard disk
   C) RAM
   D) ROM

10. Which of the following best describes integrated circuits?
   A) They use vacuum tubes.
   B) They do not contain transistors.
   C) They store analog signals.
   D) They can be small and contain many solid-state components.

Thinking Critically

11. List and describe an analog device and a digital device.

12. Copy and complete the table describing solid-state components.

Solid-State Components		
Component	Description	Use
Diode		
Transistor		
Integrated circuit		

13. Describe why the invention of integrated circuits was so important for making small, fast computers.

14. How is the binary system different from the number system you use every day? Why is the binary system used to store information in computers?

15. Describe and classify the different types of internal and external computer memory.

Developing Skills

16. **Comparing and Contrasting** How are analog and digital signals similar and how are they different?

17. Recognizing Cause and Effect How did the development of solid-state components affect electronic devices?

18. Developing Multimedia Presentations Create a multimedia presentation showing the history of computers.

19. Concept Mapping Complete the following events chain showing the sequence of events when a computer mouse is moved.

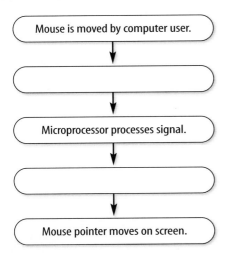

Mouse is moved by computer user.

↓

↓

Microprocessor processes signal.

↓

↓

Mouse pointer moves on screen.

Performance Assessment

20. Make a Poster Microprocessors continue to become smaller and more complex. Go to the Glencoe Science Web site at **science.glencoe.com** for more information about different microprocessors. Make a poster that explains what you learned.

TECHNOLOGY

Go to the Glencoe Science Web site at **science.glencoe.com** or use the **Glencoe Science CD-ROM** for additional chapter assessment.

Test Practice

Students at Martin Luther King, Jr. middle school were studying different computer hard disks and their storage capacities. Their information is shown in the table below.

Storage Capacity	
Hard Disk	Storage Capacity (Mb)
R	5,120
S	20,480
T	32,768
U	13,312

Study the table and answer the following questions.

1. According to this table, the storage capacity of the largest hard disk is about how many times larger than that of the smallest hard disk?
A) 3
B) 4
C) 6
D) 8

2. If a megabyte (Mb) equals 1,024 kilobytes, which hard disk has a storage capacity of about 13 million kilobytes?
F) R
G) S
H) T
J) U

Read the passage. Then read each question that follows the passage. Decide which is the best answer to each question.

Magnetic Levitation Train

One of the first things people learn about magnets is that like magnetic poles repel each other. This is the basic principle behind the Magnetic Levitation Train, or Maglev.

Maglev is a high-speed train. It uses high-strength magnets to lift and propel the train to incredible speeds as it hovers only a few centimeters above the track. This helps the train to reach higher speeds than conventional trains. A full-size Maglev in Japan achieved a speed of over 500 km/h! Its electromagnetic motor can be precisely controlled to provide smooth acceleration and braking between stops. The magnetic field prevents the train from drifting away from the center of the guideway.

Because there is no friction between wheels and rails, Maglevs eliminate the principal limitation of <u>conventional</u> trains, which is the high cost of maintaining the tracks to avoid excessive vibration and wear that can cause dangerous derailments. Critics point out that Maglevs require enormous amounts of energy. However, studies have shown that Maglevs use 30 percent less energy than other high-speed trains traveling at the same speed. Others worry about the dangers from magnetic fields; however, measurements show that humans are exposed to magnetic fields no stronger than those from toasters or hair dryers.

This year in Japan a series of Maglevs will be tested on a 43-km demonstration line. Perhaps someday Maglevs will carry commuters to and from work and school in the United States.

Test-Taking Tip After you read the passage, write a one-sentence summary of the main idea for each paragraph.

This is a Maglev test train in Japan.

1. Which of the following statements best summarizes this passage?
   - **A)** Maglev transportation is currently in use in Germany and Japan.
   - **B)** Maglev might be a high-speed transport system of the future.
   - **C)** Maglevs use more energy than conventional high-speed trains.
   - **D)** Maglevs expose passengers to strong magnetic fields.

2. In this passage, the word <u>conventional</u> means _____.
   - **F)** customary
   - **G)** innovative
   - **H)** political
   - **J)** unusual

Reasoning and Skills

Read each question and choose the best answer.

1. Voltage increases when the output coil in a transformer has more turns of wire than the input coil. Which of the following increases voltage the most?

A)

B)

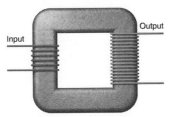

C)

D)

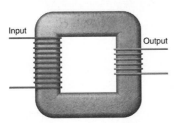

Test-Taking Tip Use the information provided in the question to closely consider each answer choice.

2. Which of the following materials would make a good conductor?
  F) plastic
  G) wood
  H) glass
  J) copper

Test-Taking Tip Remember that electrons move easily through conductors.

3. Shahid wanted to pick up pieces of metal with a magnet. Which of the following statements describes a situation in which the magnet would NOT pick up the pieces of metal?
  A) The metal pieces were too close to the magnet.
  B) The magnet was brand new.
  C) The metal pieces were made out of aluminum foil.
  D) The metal pieces and the magnet have the same magnetic poles.

Test-Taking Tip Review what you have learned about magnetic materials.

Consider this question carefully before writing your answer on a separate sheet of paper.

4. Recall what you know about the production of electric current. Explain the similarities and differences between direct current (DC) and alternating current (AC).

Test-Taking Tip Use the clues *direct* and *alternating* to guide your answer.

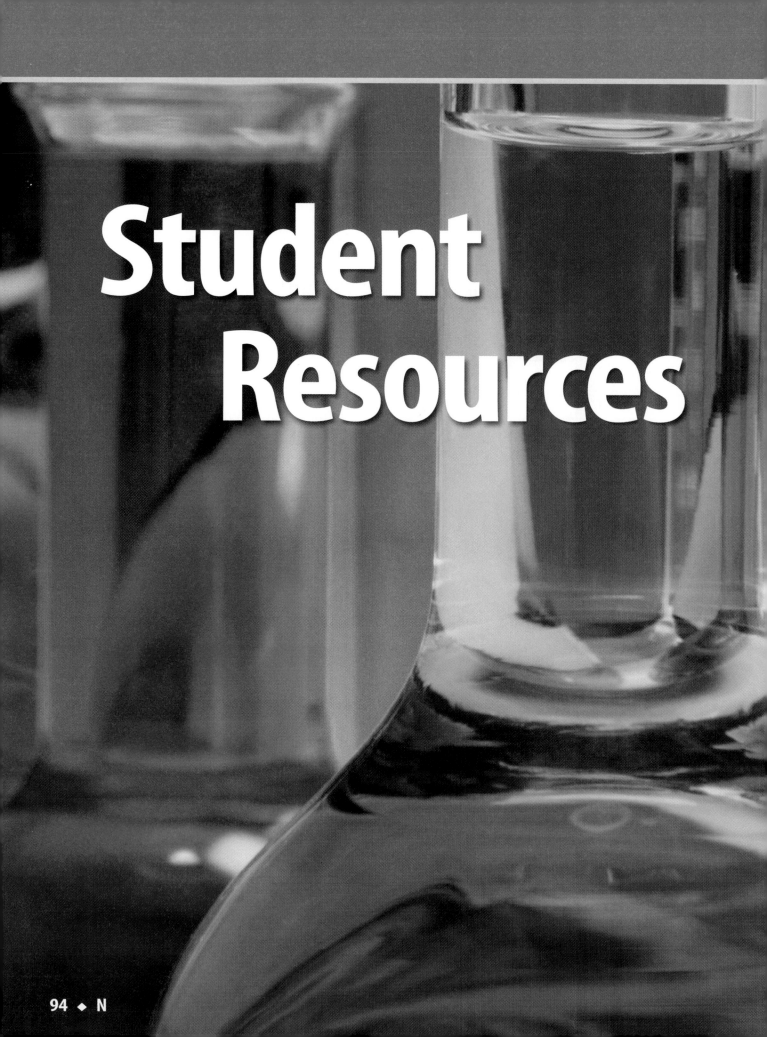

Student Resources

CONTENTS

Field GUIDE

Lightning

When storm clouds form, the particles in clouds collide with one another, removing electrons from some and adding them to others. Positive charges accumulate at the top of the cloud, leaving the negative ones at the bottom. These negative charges repel electrons in the ground below. As a result, the ground beneath the cloud becomes positively charged. The negative charges in the cloud are attracted toward the positively charged ground. They move downward in a zigzag path called a stepped leader. As the leader approaches the ground, a streamer of positive charges rises to meet it. When they meet, a return stroke—an electric spark called lightning—blasts up to the cloud.

The cycle of leader and return strokes can repeat many times in less than a second to comprise a single flash of lightning that you see.

Common Types of Lightning

The most common type of lightning strikes from one part of a cloud to another part of the same cloud. This type of lightning can occur ten times more often than lightning from a cloud to the ground. Other forms include strikes from one cloud to a different cloud, and from a cloud to the surrounding air.

Cloud-to-Ground Lightning

This type of lightning is characterized by a single streak of light connecting the cloud and the ground or a streak with one or more forks in it. Occasionally, a tall object on Earth will initiate the leader strike, causing what is known as ground-to-cloud lightning.

Cloud-to-ground lightning

Field Activity

During a thunderstorm, observe lightning from a safe location in your home or school. Using this field guide, identify and record in your Science Journal the types of lightning you saw. Also, note the date and time of the thunderstorm in your Science Journal.

Cloud-to-Cloud Lightning

Cloud-to-cloud lightning is the most common type of lightning. It can occur between clouds (intercloud lightning) or within a cloud (intracloud lightning). The lightning is often hidden by the clouds, such that the clouds themselves seem to be glowing flashes of light.

Cloud-to-Air Lightning

When a lightning stroke ends in midair above a cloud or forks off the main stroke of cloud-to-ground lightning, it causes what is known as cloud-to-air lightning. This type of lightning is usually not as powerful or as bright as cloud-to-ground lightning.

Cloud-to-air lightning

Some forms of lightning differ in appearance from the forked flashes commonly considered to be lightning. However, the discharge in the cloud occurs for the same reason—to neutralize the accumulation of charge.

Sheet lightning

Sheet Lightning

Sheet lightning appears to fill a large section of the sky. Its appearance is caused by light reflecting off the water droplets in the clouds. The actual strokes of lightning are far away or hidden by the clouds. When the lightning is so far away that no thunder is heard, it is often called heat lightning and usually can be seen during summer nights.

Ribbon Lightning

Ribbon lightning is a thicker flash than ordinary cloud-to-ground lightning. In this case, wind blows the channel that is created by the return stroke sideways. Because each return stroke follows this channel, each is moved slightly to the side of the last stroke, making each return stroke of the flash visible, and thus a wider, ribbonlike band of light is produced.

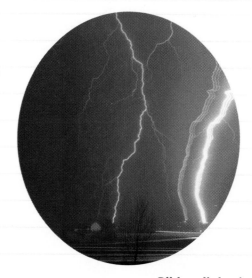

Ribbon lightning

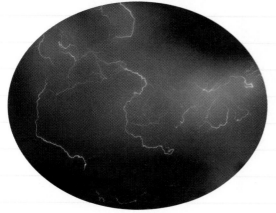

Bead lightning

Chain Lightning

Chain lightning, also called bead lightning, is distinguished by a dotted line of light as it fades. The cause is still uncertain, but it might be due to the observer's position relative to lightning or to parts of the flash being hidden by clouds or rain.

Some forms of lightning are rare or poorly understood and have different appearances than the previously described forms.

Sprites

Sprites are red or blue flashes of light that are sometimes cone shaped and occur high above a thundercloud, 60 to 100 km above Earth. The flashes are associated with thunderstorms that cover a vast area. Sprites are estimated to occur in about 1 percent of all lightning strokes.

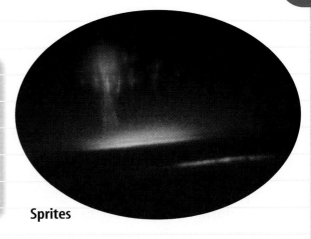

Sprites

Ball Lightning

There have been numerous eyewitness accounts of the existence of ball lightning, which appears as a sphere of red, yellow, orange or white light, usually between 1 cm to 1 m in size. Ball lightning seems to occur during thunderstorms, and appears within a few meters of the ground. The ball may move horizontally at a speed of a few meters per second, or may float in the air. Ball lightning usually lasts for several seconds and may vanish either quietly or explosively. Unlike other forms of lightning which can be seen by many observers at large distances, the small size of ball lightning and its random occurrence make it difficult to study. As a result, the causes of ball lightning still are not known, and even its existence is disputed.

St. Elmo's Fire

St. Elmo's Fire is a bluish-green glowing light that sometimes appears during thunderstorms around tall, pointed objects like the masts of ships and lightning rods. It also occurs around the wings and propellers of airplanes flying through thunderstorms. A sizzling or crackling noise often accompanies the glow. St. Elmo's Fire is caused by the strong electric field between the bottom of a thundercloud and the ground. This electric field is strongest around pointed objects. If this field is strong enough, it can pull electrons from atoms in the air. The glow is produced when these electrons collide with other atoms and molecules in the air.

As you study science, you will make many observations and conduct investigations and experiments. You will also research information that is available from many sources. These activities will involve organizing and recording data. The quality of the data you collect and the way you organize it will determine how well others can understand and use it. In **Figure 1,** the student is obtaining and recording information using a thermometer.

Putting your observations in writing is an important way of communicating to others the information you have found and the results of your investigations and experiments.

Researching Information

Scientists work to build on and add to human knowledge of the world. Before moving in a new direction, it is important to gather the information that already is known about a subject. You will look for such information in various reference sources. Follow these steps to research information on a scientific subject:

Step 1 Determine exactly what you need to know about the subject. For instance, you might want to find out about one of the elements in the periodic table.

Step 2 Make a list of questions, such as: Who discovered the element? When was it discovered? What makes the element useful or interesting?

Step 3 Use multiple sources such as textbooks, encyclopedias, government documents, professional journals, science magazines, and the Internet.

Step 4 List where you found the sources. Make sure the sources you use are reliable and the most current available.

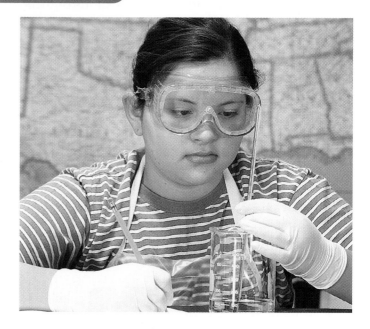

Figure 1
Making an observation is one way to gather information directly.

Evaluating Print and Nonprint Sources

Not all sources of information are reliable. Evaluate the sources you use for information, and use only those you know to be dependable. For example, suppose you want to find ways to make your home more energy efficient. You might find two Web sites on how to save energy in your home. One Web site contains "Energy-Saving Tips" written by a company that sells a new type of weatherproofing material you put around your door frames. The other is a Web page on "Conserving Energy in Your Home" written by the U.S. Department of Energy. You would choose the second Web site as the more reliable source of information.

In science, information can change rapidly. Always consult the most current sources. A 1985 source about saving energy would not reflect the most recent research and findings.

Interpreting Scientific Illustrations

As you research a science topic, you will see drawings, diagrams, and photographs. Illustrations help you understand what you read. Some illustrations are included to help you understand an idea that you can't see easily by yourself. For instance, you can't see the tiny particles in an atom, but you can look at a diagram of an atom as labeled in **Figure 2** that helps you understand something about it. Visualizing a drawing helps many people remember details more easily. Illustrations also provide examples that clarify difficult concepts or give additional information about the topic you are studying.

Most illustrations have a label or caption. A label or caption identifies the illustration or provides additional information to better explain it. Can you find the caption or labels in **Figure 2?**

Figure 2
This drawing shows an atom of carbon with its six protons, six neutrons, and six electrons.

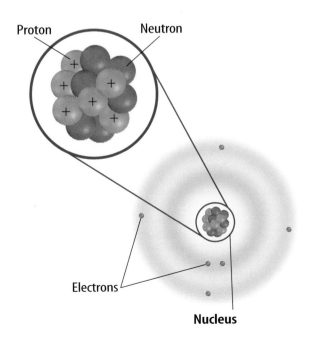

Venn Diagram

Although it is not a concept map, a Venn diagram illustrates how two subjects compare and contrast. In other words, you can see the characteristics that the subjects have in common and those that they do not.

The Venn diagram in **Figure 3** shows the relationship between two different substances made from the element carbon. However, due to the way their atoms are arranged, one substance is the gemstone diamond, and the other is the graphite found in pencils.

Concept Mapping

If you were taking a car trip, you might take some sort of road map. By using a map, you begin to learn where you are in relation to other places on the map.

A concept map is similar to a road map, but a concept map shows relationships among ideas (or concepts) rather than places. It is a diagram that visually shows how concepts are related. Because a concept map shows relationships among ideas, it can make the meanings of ideas and terms clear and help you understand what you are studying.

Overall, concept maps are useful for breaking large concepts down into smaller parts, making learning easier.

Figure 3
A Venn diagram shows how objects or concepts are alike and how they are different.

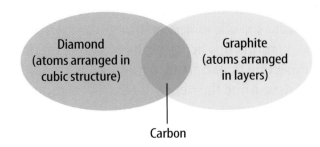

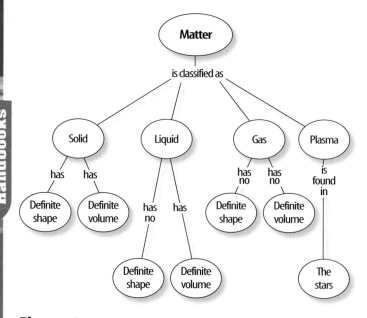

Figure 4
A network tree shows how concepts or objects are related.

Network Tree Look at the network tree in **Figure 4,** that describes the different types of matter. A network tree is a type of concept map. Notice how some words are in ovals while others are written across connecting lines. The words inside the ovals are science terms or concepts. The words written on the connecting lines describe the relationships between the concepts.

When constructing a network tree, write the topic on a note card or piece of paper. Write the major concepts related to that topic on separate note cards or pieces of paper. Then arrange them in order from general to specific. Branch the related concepts from the major concept and describe the relationships on the connecting lines. Continue branching to more specific concepts. If necessary, write the relationships between the concepts on the connecting lines until all concepts are mapped. Then examine the network tree for relationships that cross branches, and add them to the network tree.

Events Chain An events chain is another type of concept map. It models the order, or sequence, of items. In science, an events chain can be used to describe a sequence of events, the steps in a procedure, or the stages of a process.

When making an events chain, first find the one event that starts the chain. This event is called the initiating event. Then, find the next event in the chain and continue until you reach an outcome. Suppose you are asked to describe why and how a sound might make an echo. You might draw an events chain such as the one in **Figure 5.** Notice that connecting words are not necessary in an events chain.

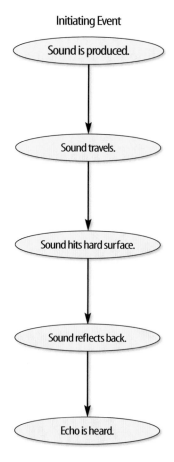

Figure 5
Events chains show the order of steps in a process or event.

Cycle Map A cycle concept map is a specific type of events chain map. In a cycle concept map, the series of events does not produce a final outcome. Instead, the last event in the chain relates back to the beginning event.

You first decide what event will be used as the beginning event. Once that is decided, you list events in order that occur after it. Words are written between events that describe what happens from one event to the next. The last event in a cycle concept map relates back to the beginning event. The number of events in a cycle concept varies, but is usually three or more. Look at the cycle map, as shown in **Figure 6.**

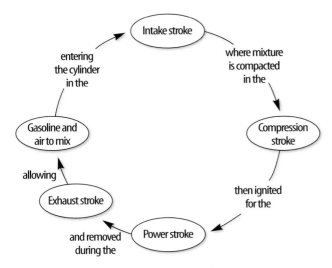

Figure 6
A cycle map shows events that occur in a cycle.

Spider Map A type of concept map that you can use for brainstorming is the spider map. When you have a central idea, you might find you have a jumble of ideas that relate to it but are not necessarily clearly related to each other. The spider map on sound in **Figure 7** shows that if you write these ideas outside the main concept, then you can begin to separate and group un-related terms so they become more useful.

Figure 7
A spider map allows you to list ideas that relate to a central topic but not necessarily to one another.

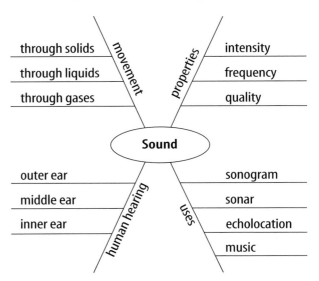

Writing a Paper

You will write papers often when researching science topics or reporting the results of investigations or experiments. Scientists frequently write papers to share their data and conclusions with other scientists and the public. When writing a paper, use these steps.

Step 1 Assemble your data by using graphs, tables, or a concept map. Create an outline.

Step 2 Start with an introduction that contains a clear statement of purpose and what you intend to discuss or prove.

Step 3 Organize the body into paragraphs. Each paragraph should start with a topic sentence, and the remaining sentences in that paragraph should support your point.

Step 4 Position data to help support your points.

Step 5 Summarize the main points and finish with a conclusion statement.

Step 6 Use tables, graphs, charts, and illustrations whenever possible.

Investigating and Experimenting

You might say the work of a scientist is to solve problems. When you decide to find out why your neighbor's hydrangeas produce blue flowers while yours are pink, you are problem solving, too. You might also observe that your neighbor's azaleas are healthier than yours are and decide to see whether differences in the soil explain the differences in these plants.

Scientists use orderly approaches to solve problems. The methods scientists use include identifying a question, making observations, forming a hypothesis, testing a hypothesis, analyzing results, and drawing conclusions.

Scientific investigations involve careful observation under controlled conditions. Such observation of an object or a process can suggest new and interesting questions about it. These questions sometimes lead to the formation of a hypothesis. Scientific investigations are designed to test a hypothesis.

Identifying a Question

The first step in a scientific investigation or experiment is to identify a question to be answered or a problem to be solved. You might be interested in knowing how beams of laser light like the ones in **Figure 8** look the way they do.

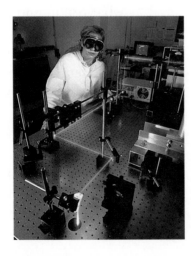

Figure 8
When you see lasers being used for scientific research, you might ask yourself, "Are these lasers different from those that are used for surgery?"

Forming Hypotheses

Hypotheses are based on observations that have been made. A hypothesis is a possible explanation based on previous knowledge and observations.

Perhaps a scientist has observed that certain substances dissolve faster in warm water than in cold. Based on these observations, the scientist can make a statement that he or she can test. The statement is a hypothesis. The hypothesis could be: *A substance dissolves in warm water faster.* A hypothesis has to be something you can test by using an investigation. A testable hypothesis is a valid hypothesis.

Predicting

When you apply a hypothesis to a specific situation, you predict something about that situation. First, you must identify which hypothesis fits the situation you are considering. People use predictions to make everyday decisions. Based on previous observations and experiences, you might form a prediction that if substances dissolve in warm water faster, then heating the water will shorten mixing time for powdered fruit drinks. Someone could use this prediction to save time in preparing a fruit punch for a party.

Testing a Hypothesis

To test a hypothesis, you need a procedure. A procedure is the plan you follow in your experiment. A procedure tells you what materials to use, as well as how and in what order to use them. When you follow a procedure, data are generated that support or do not support the original hypothesis statement.

For example, premium gasoline costs more than regular gasoline. Does premium gasoline increase the efficiency or fuel mileage of your family car? You decide to test the hypothesis: "If premium gasoline is more efficient, then it should increase the fuel mileage of my family's car." Then you write the procedure shown in **Figure 9** for your experiment and generate the data presented in the table below.

Figure 9
A procedure tells you what to do step by step.

> **Procedure**
> 1. Use regular gasoline for two weeks.
> 2. Record the number of kilometers between fill-ups and the amount of gasoline used.
> 3. Switch to premium gasoline for two weeks.
> 4. Record the number of kilometers between fill-ups and the amount of gasoline used.

Gasoline Data			
Type of Gasoline	**Kilometers Traveled**	**Liters Used**	**Liters per Kilometer**
Regular	762	45.34	0.059
Premium	661	42.30	0.064

These data show that premium gasoline is less efficient than regular gasoline in one particular car. It took more gasoline to travel 1 km (0.064) using premium gasoline than it did to travel 1 km using regular gasoline (0.059). This conclusion does not support the hypothesis.

Are all investigations alike? Keep in mind as you perform investigations in science that a hypothesis can be tested in many ways. Not every investigation makes use of all the ways that are described on these pages, and not all hypotheses are tested by investigations. Scientists encounter many variations in the methods that are used when they perform experiments. The skills in this handbook are here for you to use and practice.

Identifying and Manipulating Variables and Controls

In any experiment, it is important to keep everything the same except for the item you are testing. The one factor you change is called the independent variable. The factor that changes as a result of the independent variable is called the dependent variable. Always make sure you have only one independent variable. If you allow more than one, you will not know what causes the changes you observe in the dependent variable. Many experiments also have controls—individual instances or experimental subjects for which the independent variable is not changed. You can then compare the test results to the control results.

For example, in the fuel-mileage experiment, you made everything the same except the type of gasoline that was used. The driver, the type of automobile, and the type of driving were the same throughout. In this way, you could be sure that any mileage differences were caused by the type of fuel—the independent variable. The fuel mileage was the dependent variable.

If you could repeat the experiment using several automobiles of the same type on a standard driving track with the same driver, you could make one automobile a control by using regular gasoline over the four-week period.

Collecting Data

Whether you are carrying out an investigation or a short observational experiment, you will collect data, or information. Scientists collect data accurately as numbers and descriptions and organize it in specific ways.

Observing Scientists observe items and events, then record what they see. When they use only words to describe an observation, it is called qualitative data. For example, a scientist might describe the color, texture, or odor of a substance produced in a chemical reaction. Scientists' observations also can describe how much there is of something. These observations use numbers, as well as words, in the description and are called quantitative data. For example, if a sample of the element gold is described as being "shiny and very dense," the data are clearly qualitative. Quantitative data on this sample of gold might include "a mass of 30 g and a density of 19.3 g/cm^3." Quantitative data often are organized into tables. Then, from information in the table, a graph can be drawn. Graphs can reveal relationships that exist in experimental data.

When you make observations in science, you should examine the entire object or situation first, then look carefully for details. If you're looking at an element sample, for instance, check the general color and pattern of the sample before using a hand lens to examine its surface for any smaller details or characteristics. Remember to record accurately everything you see.

Scientists try to make careful and accurate observations. When possible, they use instruments such as microscopes, metric rulers, graduated cylinders, thermometers, and balances. Measurements provide numerical data that can be repeated and checked.

Sampling When working with large numbers of objects or a large population, scientists usually cannot observe or study every one of them. Instead, they use a sample or a portion of the total number. To *sample* is to take a small, representative portion of the objects or organisms of a population for research. By making careful observations or manipulating variables within a portion of a group, information is discovered and conclusions are drawn that might apply to the whole population.

Estimating Scientific work also involves estimating. To estimate is to make a judgment about the size or the number of something without measuring or counting every object or member of a population. Scientists first measure or count the amount or number in a small sample. A geologist, for example, might remove a 10-g sample from a large rock that is rich in copper ore, as in **Figure 10.** Then a chemist would determine the percentage of copper by mass and multiply that percentage by the total mass of the rock to estimate the total mass of copper in the large rock.

Figure 10
Determining the percentage of copper by mass that is present in a small piece of a large rock, which is rich in copper ore, can help estimate the total mass of copper ore that is present in the rock.

Measuring in SI

The metric system of measurement was developed in 1795. A modern form of the metric system, called the International System, or SI, was adopted in 1960. SI provides standard measurements that all scientists around the world can understand.

The metric system is convenient because unit sizes vary by multiples of 10. When changing from smaller units to larger units, divide by a multiple of 10. When changing from larger units to smaller, multiply by a multiple of 10. To convert millimeters to centimeters, divide the millimeters by 10. To convert 30 mm to centimeters, divide 30 by 10 (30 mm equal 3 cm).

Prefixes are used to name units. Look at the table below for some common metric prefixes and their meanings. Do you see how the prefix *kilo-* attached to the unit *gram* is *kilogram*, or 1,000 g?

Metric Prefixes			
Prefix	**Symbol**	**Meaning**	
kilo-	k	1,000	thousand
hecto-	h	100	hundred
deka-	da	10	ten
deci-	d	0.1	tenth
centi-	c	0.01	hundredth
milli-	m	0.001	thousandth

Now look at the metric ruler shown in **Figure 11.** The centimeter lines are the long, numbered lines, and the shorter lines are millimeter lines.

When using a metric ruler, line up the 0-cm mark with the end of the object being measured, and read the number of the unit where the object ends, in this instance it would be 4.5 cm.

Figure 11
This metric ruler has centimeter and millimeter divisions.

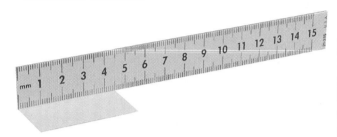

Liquid Volume In some science activities, you will measure liquids. The unit that is used to measure liquids is the liter. A liter has the volume of 1,000 cm³. The prefix *milli-* means "thousandth (0.001)." A milliliter is one thousandth of 1 L, and 1 L has the volume of 1,000 mL. One milliliter of liquid completely fills a cube measuring 1 cm on each side. Therefore, 1 mL equals 1 cm³.

You will use beakers and graduated cylinders to measure liquid volume. A graduated cylinder, as illustrated in **Figure 12,** is marked from bottom to top in milliliters. This one contains 79 mL of a liquid.

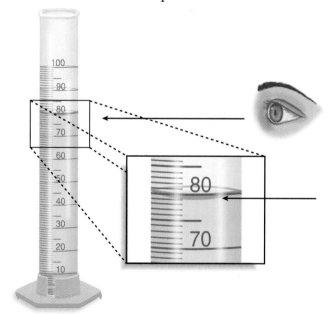

Figure 12
Graduated cylinders measure liquid volume.

Mass Scientists measure mass in grams. You might use a beam balance similar to the one shown in **Figure 13.** The balance has a pan on one side and a set of beams on the other side. Each beam has a rider that slides on the beam.

Before you find the mass of an object, slide all the riders back to the zero point. Check the pointer on the right to make sure it swings an equal distance above and below the zero point. If the swing is unequal, find and turn the adjusting screw until you have an equal swing.

Place an object on the pan. Slide the largest rider along its beam until the pointer drops below zero. Then move it back one notch. Repeat the process on each beam until the pointer swings an equal distance above and below the zero point. Sum the masses on each beam to find the mass of the object. Move all riders back to zero when finished.

Figure 13
A triple beam balance is used to determine the mass of an object.

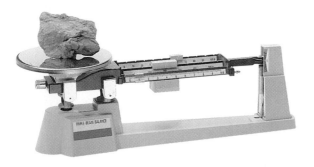

You should never place a hot object on the pan or pour chemicals directly onto the pan. Instead, find the mass of a clean container. Remove the container from the pan, then place the chemicals in the container. Find the mass of the container with the chemicals in it. To find the mass of the chemicals, subtract the mass of the empty container from the mass of the filled container.

Making and Using Tables

Browse through your textbook and you will see tables in the text and in the activities. In a table, data, or information, are arranged so that they are easier to understand. Activity tables help organize the data you collect during an activity so results can be interpreted.

Making Tables To make a table, list the items to be compared in the first column and the characteristics to be compared in the first row. The title should clearly indicate the content of the table, and the column or row heads should tell the reader what information is found in there. The table below lists materials collected for recycling on three weekly pick-up days. The inclusion of kilograms in parentheses also identifies for the reader that the figures are mass units.

Recyclable Materials Collected During Week			
Day of Week	Paper (kg)	Aluminum (kg)	Glass (kg)
Monday	5.0	4.0	12.0
Wednesday	4.0	1.0	10.0
Friday	2.5	2.0	10.0

Using Tables How much paper, in kilograms, is being recycled on Wednesday? Locate the column labeled "Paper (kg)" and the row "Wednesday." The information in the box where the column and row intersect is the answer. Did you answer "4.0"? How much aluminum, in kilograms, is being recycled on Friday? If you answered "2.0," you understand how to read the table. How much glass is collected for recycling each week? Locate the column labeled "Glass (kg)" and add the figures for all three rows. If you answered "32.0," then you know how to locate and use the data provided in the table.

Recording Data

To be useful, the data you collect must be recorded carefully. Accuracy is key. A well-thought-out experiment includes a way to record procedures, observations, and results accurately. Data tables are one way to organize and record results. Set up the tables you will need ahead of time so you can record the data right away.

Record information properly and neatly. Never put unidentified data on scraps of paper. Instead, data should be written in a notebook like the one in **Figure 14.** Write in pencil so information isn't lost if your data get wet. At each point in the experiment, record your information and label it. That way, your data will be accurate and you will not have to determine what the figures mean when you look at your notes later.

Figure 14
Record data neatly and clearly so they are easy to understand.

Recording Observations

It is important to record observations accurately and completely. That is why you always should record observations in your notes immediately as you make them. It is easy to miss details or make mistakes when recording results from memory. Do not include your personal thoughts when you record your data. Record only what you observe to eliminate bias. For example, when you record the time required for five students to climb the same set of stairs, you would note which student took the longest time. However, you would not refer to that student's time as "the worst time of all the students in the group."

Making Models

You can organize the observations and other data you collect and record in many ways. Making models is one way to help you better understand the parts of a structure you have been observing or the way a process for which you have been taking various measurements works.

Models often show things that are too large or too small for normal viewing. For example, you normally won't see the inside of an atom. However, you can understand the structure of the atom better by making a three-dimensional model of an atom. The relative sizes, the positions, and the movements of protons, neutrons, and electrons can be explained in words. An atomic model made of a plastic-ball nucleus and pipe-cleaner electron shells can help you visualize how the parts of the atom relate to each other.

Other models can be devised on a computer. Some models, such as those that illustrate the chemical combinations of different elements, are mathematical and are represented by equations.

Making and Using Graphs

After scientists organize data in tables, they might display the data in a graph that shows the relationship of one variable to another. A graph makes interpretation and analysis of data easier. Three types of graphs are the line graph, the bar graph, and the circle graph.

Line Graphs
A line graph like in **Figure 15** is used to show the relationship between two variables. The variables being compared go on two axes of the graph. For data from an experiment, the independent variable always goes on the horizontal axis, called the *x*-axis. The dependent variable always goes on the vertical axis, called the *y*-axis. After drawing your axes, label each with a scale. Next, plot the data points.

A data point is the intersection of the recorded value of the dependent variable for each tested value of the independent variable. After all the points are plotted, connect them.

Distance v. Time

Figure 15
This line graph shows the relationship between distance and time during a bicycle ride lasting several hours.

Bar Graphs
Bar graphs compare data that do not change continuously. Vertical bars show the relationships among data.

To make a bar graph, set up the *y*-axis as you did for the line graph. Draw vertical bars of equal size from the *x*-axis up to the point on the *y*-axis that represents the value of *x*.

Figure 16
The amount of aluminum collected for recycling during one week can be shown as a bar graph or circle graph.

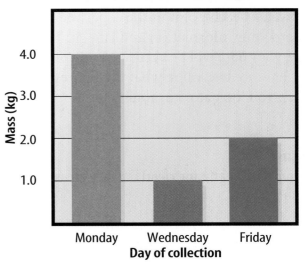

Aluminum Collected During Week

Circle Graphs
A circle graph uses a circle divided into sections to display data as parts (fractions or percentages) of a whole. The size of each section corresponds to the fraction or percentage of the data that the section represents. So, the entire circle represents 100 percent, one-half represents 50 percent, one-fifth represents 20 percent, and so on.

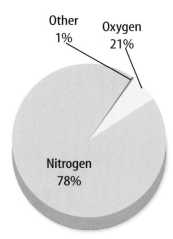

Analyzing Results

To determine the meaning of your observations and investigation results, you will need to look for patterns in the data. You can organize your information in several of the ways that are discussed in this handbook. Then you must think critically to determine what the data mean. Scientists use several approaches when they analyze the data they have collected and recorded. Each approach is useful for identifying specific patterns in the data.

Forming Operational Definitions

An operational definition defines an object by showing how it functions, works, or behaves. Such definitions are written in terms of how an object works or how it can be used; that is, they describe its job or purpose.

For example, a ruler can be defined as a tool that measures the length of an object (how it can be used). A ruler also can be defined as something that contains a series of marks that can be used as a standard when measuring (how it works).

Classifying

Classifying is the process of sorting objects or events into groups based on common features. When classifying, first observe the objects or events to be classified. Then select one feature that is shared by some members in the group but not by all. Place those members that share that feature into a subgroup. You can classify members into smaller and smaller subgroups based on characteristics.

How might you classify a group of chemicals? You might first classify them by state of matter, putting solids, liquids, and gases into separate groups. Within each group, you could then look for another common feature by which to further classify members of the group, such as color or how reactive they are.

Remember that when you classify, you are grouping objects or events for a purpose. For example, classifying chemicals can be the first step in organizing them for storage. Both at home and at school, poisonous or highly reactive chemicals should all be stored in a safe location where they are not easily accessible to small children or animals. Solids, liquids, and gases each have specific storage requirements that may include waterproof, airtight, or pressurized containers. Are the dangerous chemicals in your home stored in the right place? Keep your purpose in mind as you select the features to form groups and subgroups.

Figure 17
Color is one of many characteristics that are used to classify chemicals.

Comparing and Contrasting

Observations can be analyzed by noting the similarities and differences between two or more objects or events that you observe. When you look at objects or events to see how they are similar, you are comparing them. Contrasting is looking for differences in objects or events. The table below compares and contrasts the characteristics of two elements.

Elemental Characteristics		
Element	Aluminum	Gold
Color	silver	gold
Classification	metal	metal
Density (g/cm^3)	2.7	19.3
Melting Point (°C)	660	1064

Recognizing Cause and Effect

Have you ever heard a loud pop right before the power went out and then suggested that an electric transformer probably blew out? If so, you have observed an effect and inferred a cause. The event is the effect, and the reason for the event is the cause.

When scientists are unsure of the cause of a certain event, they design controlled experiments to determine what caused it.

Interpreting Data

The word *interpret* means "to explain the meaning of something." Look at the problem originally being explored in an experiment and figure out what the data show. Identify the control group and the test group so you can see whether or not changes in the independent variable have had an effect. Look for differences in the dependent variable between the control and test groups.

These differences you observe can be qualitative or quantitative. You would be able to describe a qualitative difference using only words, whereas you would measure a quantitative difference and describe it using numbers. If there are differences, the independent variable that is being tested could have had an effect. If no differences are found between the control and test groups, the variable that is being tested apparently had no effect.

For example, suppose that three beakers each contain 100 mL of water. The beakers are placed on hot plates, and two of the hot plates are turned on, but the third is left off for a period of 5 min. Suppose you are then asked to describe any differences in the water in the three beakers. A qualitative difference might be the appearance of bubbles rising to the top in the water that is being heated but no rising bubbles in the unheated water. A quantitative difference might be a difference in the amount of water that is present in the beakers.

Inferring Scientists often make inferences based on their observations. An inference is an attempt to explain, or interpret, observations or to indicate what caused what you observed. An inference is a type of conclusion.

When making an inference, be certain to use accurate data and accurately described observations. Analyze all of the data that you've collected. Then, based on everything you know, explain or interpret what you've observed.

Drawing Conclusions

When scientists have analyzed the data they collected, they proceed to draw conclusions about what the data mean. These conclusions are sometimes stated using words similar to those found in the hypothesis formed earlier in the process.

Conclusions To analyze your data, you must review all of the observations and measurements that you made and recorded. Recheck all data for accuracy. After your data are rechecked and organized, you are almost ready to draw a conclusion such as "salt water boils at a higher temperature than freshwater."

Before you can draw a conclusion, however, you must determine whether the data allow you to come to a conclusion that supports a hypothesis. Sometimes that will be the case, other times it will not.

If your data do not support a hypothesis, it does not mean that the hypothesis is wrong. It means only that the results of the investigation did not support the hypothesis. Maybe the experiment needs to be redesigned, but very likely, some of the initial observations on which the hypothesis was based were incomplete or biased. Perhaps more observation or research is needed to refine the hypothesis.

Avoiding Bias Sometimes drawing a conclusion involves making judgments. When you make a judgment, you form an opinion about what your data mean. It is important to be honest and to avoid reaching a conclusion if no supporting evidence for it exists or if it was based on a small sample. It also is important not to allow any expectations of results to bias your judgments. If possible, it is a good idea to collect additional data. Scientists do this all the time.

For example, the *Hubble Space Telescope* was sent into space in April, 1990, to provide scientists with clearer views of the universe. *Hubble* is the size of a school bus and has a 2.4-m-diameter mirror. *Hubble* helped scientists answer questions about the planet Pluto.

For many years, scientists had only been able to hypothesize about the surface of the planet Pluto. *Hubble* has now provided pictures of Pluto's surface that show a rough texture with light and dark regions on it. This might be the best information about Pluto scientists will have until they are able to send a space probe to it.

Evaluating Others' Data and Conclusions

Sometimes scientists have to use data that they did not collect themselves, or they have to rely on observations and conclusions drawn by other researchers. In cases such as these, the data must be evaluated carefully.

How were the data obtained? How was the investigation done? Was it carried out properly? Has it been duplicated by other researchers? Were they able to follow the exact procedure? Did they come up with the same results? Look at the conclusion, as well. Would you reach the same conclusion from these results? Only when you have confidence in the data of others can you believe it is true and feel comfortable using it.

Communicating

The communication of ideas is an important part of the work of scientists. A discovery that is not reported will not advance the scientific community's understanding or knowledge. Communication among scientists also is important as a way of improving their investigations.

Scientists communicate in many ways, from writing articles in journals and magazines that explain their investigations and experiments, to announcing important discoveries on television and radio, to sharing ideas with colleagues on the Internet or presenting them as lectures.

People who study science rely on computers to record and store data and to analyze results from investigations. Whether you work in a laboratory or just need to write a lab report with tables, good computer skills are a necessity.

Using a Word Processor

Suppose your teacher has assigned a written report. After you've completed your research and decided how you want to write the information, you need to put all that information on paper. The easiest way to do this is with a word processing application on a computer.

A computer application that allows you to type your information, change it as many times as you need to, and then print it out so that it looks neat and clean is called a word processing application. You also can use this type of application to create tables and columns, add bullets or cartoon art to your page, include page numbers, and check your spelling.

Helpful Hints

- If you aren't sure how to do something using your word processing program, look in the help menu. You will find a list of topics there to click on for help. After you locate the help topic you need, just follow the step-by-step instructions you see on your screen.
- Just because you've spell checked your report doesn't mean that the spelling is perfect. The spell check feature can't catch misspelled words that look like other words. If you've accidentally typed *cold* instead of *gold*, the spell checker won't know the difference. Always reread your report to make sure you didn't miss any mistakes.

Figure 18
You can use computer programs to make graphs and tables.

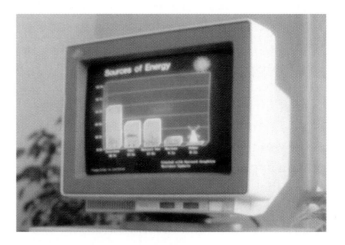

Using a Database

Imagine you're in the middle of a research project, busily gathering facts and information. You soon realize that it's becoming more difficult to organize and keep track of all the information. The tool to use to solve information overload is a database. Just as a file cabinet organizes paper records, a database organizes computer records. However, a database is more powerful than a simple file cabinet because at the click of a mouse, the contents can be reshuffled and reorganized. At computer-quick speeds, databases can sort information by any characteristics and filter data into multiple categories.

Helpful Hints

- Before setting up a database, take some time to learn the features of your database software by practicing with established database software.
- Periodically save your database as you enter data. That way, if something happens such as your computer malfunctions or the power goes off, you won't lose all of your work.

Doing a Database Search

When searching for information in a database, use the following search strategies to get the best results. These are the same search methods used for searching internet databases.

- Place the word *and* between two words in your search if you want the database to look for any entries that have both the words. For example, "gold *and* silver" would give you information that mentions both gold and silver.
- Place the word *or* between two words if you want the database to show entries that have at least one of the words. For example "gold *or* silver" would show you information that mentions either gold or silver.
- Place the word *not* between two words if you want the database to look for entries that have the first word but do not have the second word. For example, "gold *not* jewelry" would show you information that mentions gold but does not mention jewelry.

In summary, databases can be used to store large amounts of information about a particular subject. Databases allow biologists, Earth scientists, and physical scientists to search for information quickly and accurately.

Using an Electronic Spreadsheet

Your science fair experiment has produced lots of numbers. How do you keep track of all the data, and how can you easily work out all the calculations needed? You can use a computer program called a spreadsheet to record data that involve numbers. A spreadsheet is an electronic mathematical worksheet.

Type your data in rows and columns, just as they would look in a data table on a sheet of paper. A spreadsheet uses simple math to do data calculations. For example, you could add, subtract, divide, or multiply any of the values in the spreadsheet by another number. You also could set up a series of math steps you want to apply to the data. If you want to add 12 to all the numbers and then multiply all the numbers by 10, the computer does all the calculations for you in the spreadsheet. Below is an example of a spreadsheet that records test car data.

Helpful Hints

- Before you set up the spreadsheet, identify how you want to organize the data. Include any formulas you will need to use.
- Make sure you have entered the correct data into the correct rows and columns.
- You also can display your results in a graph. Pick the style of graph that best represents the data with which you are working.

Figure 19
A spreadsheet allows you to display large amounts of data and do calculations automatically.

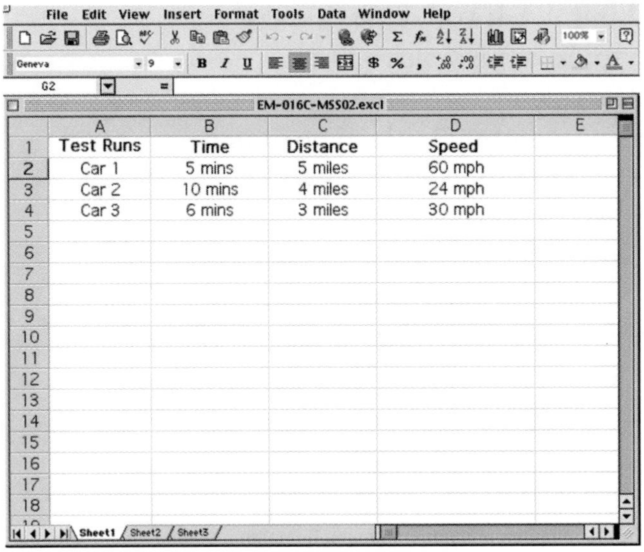

Using a Computerized Card Catalog

When you have a report or paper to research, you probably go to the library. To find the information you need in the library, you might have to use a computerized card catalog. This type of card catalog allows you to search for information by subject, by title, or by author. The computer then will display all the holdings the library has on the subject, title, or author requested.

A library's holdings can include books, magazines, databases, videos, and audio materials. When you have chosen something from this list, the computer will show whether an item is available and where in the library to find it.

Helpful Hints

- Remember that you can use the computer to search by subject, author, or title. If you know a book's author but not the title, you can search for all the books the library has by that author.
- When searching by subject, it's often most helpful to narrow your search by using specific search terms, such as *and, or,* and *not.* If you don't find enough sources this way, you can broaden your search.
- Pay attention to the type of materials found in your search. If you need a book, you can eliminate any videos or other resources that come up in your search.
- Knowing how your library is arranged can save you a lot of time. If you need help, the librarian will show you where certain types of materials are kept and how to find specific holdings.

Using Graphics Software

Are you having trouble finding that exact piece of art you're looking for? Do you have a picture in your mind of what you want but can't seem to find the right graphic to represent your ideas? To solve these problems, you can use graphics software. Graphics software allows you to create and change images and diagrams in almost unlimited ways. Typical uses for graphics software include arranging clip art, changing scanned images, and constructing pictures from scratch. Most graphics software applications work in similar ways. They use the same basic tools and functions. Once you master one graphics application, you can use other graphics applications.

Figure 20
Graphics software can use your data to draw bar graphs.

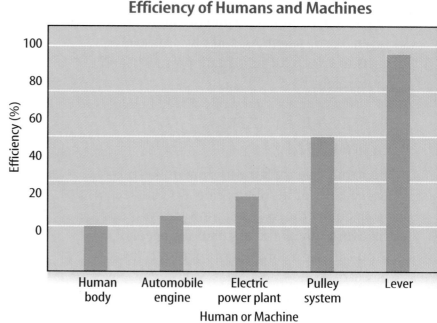

Efficiency of Humans and Machines

Figure 21
Graphics software can use your data to draw circle graphs.

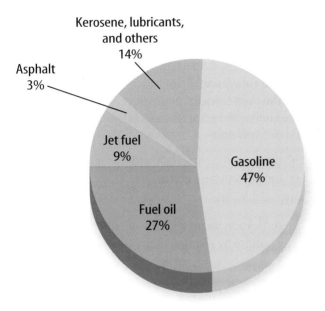

Kerosene, lubricants, and others 14%

Asphalt 3%

Jet fuel 9%

Gasoline 47%

Fuel oil 27%

First, determine what important points you want to make in your presentation. Then, write an outline of what materials and types of media would best illustrate those points. Maybe you could start with an outline on an overhead projector, then show a video, followed by something from the Internet or a slide show accompanied by music or recorded voices. You might choose to use a presentation builder computer application that can combine all these elements into one presentation. Make sure the presentation is well constructed to make the most impact on the audience.

Figure 22
Multimedia presentations use many types of print and electronic materials.

Helpful Hints
- As with any method of drawing, the more you practice using the graphics software, the better your results will be.
- Start by using the software to manipulate existing drawings. Once you master this, making your own illustrations will be easier.
- Clip art is available on CD-ROMs and the Internet. With these resources, finding a piece of clip art to suit your purposes is simple.
- As you work on a drawing, save it often.

Developing Multimedia Presentations

It's your turn—you have to present your science report to the entire class. How do you do it? You can use many different sources of information to get the class excited about your presentation. Posters, videos, photographs, sound, computers, and the Internet can help show your ideas.

Helpful Hints
- Carefully consider what media will best communicate the point you are trying to make.
- Make sure you know how to use any equipment you will be using in your presentation.
- Practice the presentation several times.
- If possible, set up all of the equipment ahead of time. Make sure everything is working correctly.

Math Skill Handbook

Use this Math Skill Handbook to help solve problems you are given in this text. You might find it useful to review topics in this Math Skill Handbook first.

Converting Units

In science, quantities such as length, mass, and time sometimes are measured using different units. Suppose you want to know how many miles are in 12.7 km.

Conversion factors are used to change from one unit of measure to another. A conversion factor is a ratio that is equal to one. For example, there are 1,000 mL in 1 L, so 1,000 mL equals 1 L, or:

$$1,000 \text{ mL} = 1 \text{ L}$$

If both sides are divided by 1 L, this equation becomes:

$$\frac{1,000 \text{ mL}}{1 \text{ L}} = 1$$

The **ratio** on the left side of this equation is equal to 1 and is a conversion factor. You can make another conversion factor by dividing both sides of the top equation by 1,000 mL:

$$1 = \frac{1 \text{ L}}{1,000 \text{ mL}}$$

To **convert units,** you multiply by the appropriate conversion factor. For example, how many milliliters are in 1.255 L? To convert 1.255 L to milliliters, multiply 1.255 L by a conversion factor.

Use the **conversion factor** with new units (mL) in the numerator and the old units (L) in the denominator.

$$1.255 \text{ L} \times \frac{1,000 \text{ mL}}{1 \text{ L}} = 1,255 \text{ mL}$$

The unit L divides in this equation, just as if it were a number.

Example 1 There are 2.54 cm in 1 inch. If a meterstick has a length of 100 cm, how long is the meterstick in inches?

Step 1 Decide which conversion factor to use. You know the length of the meterstick in centimeters, so centimeters are the old units. You want to find the length in inches, so inch is the new unit.

Step 2 Form the conversion factor. Start with the relationship between the old and new units.

$$2.54 \text{ cm} = 1 \text{ inch}$$

Step 3 Form the conversion factor with the old unit (centimeter) on the bottom by dividing both sides by 2.54 cm.

$$1 = \frac{2.54 \text{ cm}}{2.54 \text{ cm}} = \frac{1 \text{ inch}}{2.54 \text{ cm}}$$

Step 4 Multiply the old measurement by the conversion factor.

$$100 \text{ cm} \times \frac{1 \text{ inch}}{2.54 \text{ cm}} = 39.37 \text{ inches}$$

The meterstick is 39.37 inches long.

Example 2 There are 365 days in one year. If a person is 14 years old, what is his or her age in days? (Ignore leap years)

Step 1 Decide which conversion factor to use. You want to convert years to days.

Step 2 Form the conversion factor. Start with the relation between the old and new units.

$$1 \text{ year} = 365 \text{ days}$$

Step 3 Form the conversion factor with the old unit (year) on the bottom by dividing both sides by 1 year.

$$1 = \frac{1 \text{ year}}{1 \text{ year}} = \frac{365 \text{ days}}{1 \text{ year}}$$

Step 4 Multiply the old measurement by the conversion factor:

$$14 \text{ years} \times \frac{365 \text{ days}}{1 \text{ year}} = 5,110 \text{ days}$$

The person's age is 5,110 days.

Practice Problem A book has a mass of 2.31 kg. If there are 1,000 g in 1 kg, what is the mass of the book in grams?

Using Fractions

A **fraction** is a number that compares a part to the whole. For example, in the fraction $\frac{2}{3}$, the 2 represents the part and the 3 represents the whole. In the fraction $\frac{2}{3}$, the top number, 2, is called the numerator. The bottom number, 3, is called the denominator.

Sometimes fractions are not written in their simplest form. To determine a fraction's **simplest form,** you must find the greatest common factor (GCF) of the numerator and denominator. The greatest common factor is the largest factor that is common to the numerator and denominator.

For example, because the number 3 divides into 12 and 30 evenly, it is a common factor of 12 and 30. However, because the number 6 is the largest number that evenly divides into 12 and 30, it is the **greatest common factor.**

After you find the greatest common factor, you can write a fraction in its simplest form. Divide both the numerator and the denominator by the greatest common factor. The number that results is the fraction in its **simplest form.**

Example Twelve of the 20 chemicals used in the science lab are in powder form. What fraction of the chemicals used in the lab are in powder form?

Step 1 Write the fraction.

$$\frac{part}{whole} = \frac{12}{20}$$

Step 2 To find the GCF of the numerator and denominator, list all of the factors of each number.

Factors of 12: 1, 2, 3, 4, 6, 12 (the numbers that divide evenly into 12)

Factors of 20: 1, 2, 4, 5, 10, 20 (the numbers that divide evenly into 20)

Step 3 List the common factors.

1, 2, 4.

Step 4 Choose the greatest factor in the list of common factors.

The GCF of 12 and 20 is 4.

Step 5 Divide the numerator and denominator by the GCF.

$$\frac{12 \div 4}{20 \div 4} = \frac{3}{5}$$

In the lab, $\frac{3}{5}$ of the chemicals are in powder form.

Practice Problem There are 90 rides at an amusement park. Of those rides, 66 have a height restriction. What fraction of the rides has a height restriction? Write the fraction in simplest form.

Math Skill Handbook

Calculating Ratios

A **ratio** is a comparison of two numbers by division.

Ratios can be written 3 to 5 or 3:5. Ratios also can be written as fractions, such as $\frac{3}{5}$. Ratios, like fractions, can be written in simplest form. Recall that a fraction is in **simplest form** when the greatest common factor (GCF) of the numerator and denominator is 1.

Example A chemical solution contains 40 g of salt and 64 g of baking soda. What is the ratio of salt to baking soda as a fraction in simplest form?

Step 1 Write the ratio as a fraction. $\frac{\text{salt}}{\text{baking soda}} = \frac{40}{64}$

Step 2 Express the fraction in simplest form. The GCF of 40 and 64 is 8.

$$\frac{40}{64} = \frac{40 \div 8}{64 \div 8} = \frac{5}{8}$$

The ratio of salt to baking soda in the solution is $\frac{5}{8}$.

Practice Problem Two metal rods measure 100 cm and 144 cm in length. What is the ratio of their lengths in simplest fraction form?

Using Decimals

A **decimal** is a fraction with a denominator of 10, 100, 1,000, or another power of 10. For example, 0.854 is the same as the fraction $\frac{854}{1,000}$.

In a decimal, the decimal point separates the ones place and the tenths place. For example, 0.27 means twenty-seven hundredths, or $\frac{27}{100}$, where 27 is the **number of units** out of 100 units. Any fraction can be written as a decimal using division.

Example Write $\frac{5}{8}$ as a decimal.

Step 1 Write a division problem with the numerator, 5, as the dividend and the denominator, 8, as the divisor. Write 5 as 5.000.

Step 2 Solve the problem.

```
      0.625
   8)5.000
     48
     ──
     20
     16
     ──
      40
      40
      ──
       0
```

Therefore, $\frac{5}{8}$ = 0.625.

Practice Problem Write $\frac{19}{25}$ as a decimal.

Using Percentages

The word *percent* means "out of one hundred." A **percent** is a ratio that compares a number to 100. Suppose you read that 77 percent of Earth's surface is covered by water. That is the same as reading that the fraction of Earth's surface covered by water is $\frac{77}{100}$. To express a fraction as a percent, first find an equivalent decimal for the fraction. Then, multiply the decimal by 100 and add the percent symbol. For example, $\frac{1}{2} = 1 \div 2 = 0.5$. Then $0.5 \cdot 100 = 50 = 50\%$.

Example Express $\frac{13}{20}$ as a percent.

Step 1 Find the equivalent decimal for the fraction.

$$\begin{array}{r} 0.65 \\ 20\overline{)13.00} \\ \underline{12\,0} \\ 100 \\ \underline{100} \\ 0 \end{array}$$

Step 2 Rewrite the fraction $\frac{13}{20}$ as 0.65.

Step 3 Multiply 0.65 by 100 and add the % sign.

$$0.65 \cdot 100 = 65 = 65\%$$

So, $\frac{13}{20} = 65\%$.

Practice Problem In one year, 73 of 365 days were rainy in one city. What percent of the days in that city were rainy?

Using Precision and Significant Digits

When you make a **measurement,** the value you record depends on the precision of the measuring instrument. When adding or subtracting numbers with different precision, the answer is rounded to the smallest number of decimal places of any number in the sum or difference. When multiplying or dividing, the answer is rounded to the smallest number of significant figures of any number being multiplied or divided. When counting the number of **significant figures,** all digits are counted except zeros at the end of a number with no decimal such as 2,500, and zeros at the beginning of a decimal such as 0.03020.

Example The lengths 5.28 and 5.2 are measured in meters. Find the sum of these lengths and report the sum using the least precise measurement.

Step 1 Find the sum.

$$\begin{array}{ll} 5.28 \text{ m} & \text{2 digits after the decimal} \\ \underline{+\ 5.2\ \text{ m}} & \text{1 digit after the decimal} \\ 10.48 \text{ m} \end{array}$$

Step 2 Round to one digit after the decimal because the least number of digits after the decimal of the numbers being added is 1.

The sum is 10.5 m.

Practice Problem Multiply the numbers in the example using the rule for multiplying and dividing. Report the answer with the correct number of significant figures.

Math Skill Handbook

An **equation** is a statement that two things are equal. For example, $A = B$ is an equation that states that A is equal to B.

Sometimes one side of the equation will contain a **variable** whose value is not known. In the equation $3x = 12$, the variable is x.

The equation is solved when the variable is replaced with a value that makes both sides of the equation equal to each other. For example, the solution of the equation $3x = 12$ is $x = 4$. If the x is replaced with 4, then the equation becomes $3 \cdot 4 = 12$, or $12 = 12$.

To solve an equation such as $8x = 40$, divide both sides of the equation by the number that multiplies the variable.

$$8x = 40$$
$$\frac{8x}{8} = \frac{40}{8}$$
$$x = 5$$

You can check your answer by replacing the variable with your solution and seeing if both sides of the equation are the same.

$$8x = 8 \cdot 5 = 40$$

The left and right sides of the equation are the same, so $x = 5$ is the solution.

Sometimes an equation is written in this way: $a = bc$. This also is called a **formula.** The letters can be replaced by numbers, but the numbers must still make both sides of the equation the same.

Example 1 Solve the equation $10x = 35$.

Step 1 Find the solution by dividing each side of the equation by 10.

$$10x = 35 \qquad \frac{10x}{10} = \frac{35}{10} \qquad x = 3.5$$

Step 2 Check the solution.

$$10x = 35 \qquad 10 \times 3.5 = 35 \qquad 35 = 35$$

Both sides of the equation are equal, so $x = 3.5$ is the solution to the equation.

Example 2 In the formula $a = bc$, find the value of c if $a = 20$ and $b = 2$.

Step 1 Rearrange the formula so the unknown value is by itself on one side of the equation by dividing both sides by b.

$$a = bc$$
$$\frac{a}{b} = \frac{bc}{b}$$
$$\frac{a}{b} = c$$

Step 2 Replace the variables a and b with the values that are given.

$$\frac{a}{b} = c$$
$$\frac{20}{2} = c$$
$$10 = c$$

Step 3 Check the solution.

$$a = bc$$
$$20 = 2 \times 10$$
$$20 = 20$$

Both sides of the equation are equal, so $c = 10$ is the solution when $a = 20$ and $b = 2$.

Practice Problem In the formula $h = gd$, find the value of d if $g = 12.3$ and $h = 17.4$.

Using Proportions

A **proportion** is an equation that shows that two ratios are equivalent. The ratios $\frac{2}{4}$ and $\frac{5}{10}$ are equivalent, so they can be written as $\frac{2}{4} = \frac{5}{10}$. This equation is an example of a proportion.

When two ratios form a proportion, the **cross products** are equal. To find the cross products in the proportion $\frac{2}{4} = \frac{5}{10}$, multiply the 2 and the 10, and the 4 and the 5. Therefore $2 \cdot 10 = 4 \cdot 5$, **or 20 = 20.**

Because you know that both proportions are equal, you can use cross products to find a missing term in a proportion. This is known as **solving the proportion.** Solving a proportion is similar to solving an equation.

Example The heights of a tree and a pole are proportional to the lengths of their shadows. The tree casts a shadow of 24 m at the same time that a 6-m pole casts a shadow of 4 m. What is the height of the tree?

Step 1 Write a proportion.

$$\frac{\text{height of tree}}{\text{height of pole}} = \frac{\text{length of tree's shadow}}{\text{length of pole's shadow}}$$

Step 2 Substitute the known values into the proportion. Let h represent the unknown value, the height of the tree.

$$\frac{h}{6} = \frac{24}{4}$$

Step 3 Find the cross products.

$$h \cdot 4 = 6 \cdot 24$$

Step 4 Simplify the equation.

$$4h = 144$$

Step 5 Divide each side by 4.

$$\frac{4h}{4} = \frac{144}{4}$$

$$h = 36$$

The height of the tree is 36 m.

Practice Problem The ratios of the weights of two objects on the Moon and on Earth are in proportion. A rock weighing 3 N on the Moon weighs 18 N on Earth. How much would a rock that weighs 5 N on the Moon weigh on Earth?

Math Skill Handbook

Using Statistics

Statistics is the branch of mathematics that deals with collecting, analyzing, and presenting data. In statistics, there are three common ways to summarize the data with a single number—the mean, the median, and the mode.

The **mean** of a set of data is the arithmetic average. It is found by adding the numbers in the data set and dividing by the number of items in the set.

The **median** is the middle number in a set of data when the data are arranged in numerical order. If there were an even number of data points, the median would be the mean of the two middle numbers.

The **mode** of a set of data is the number or item that appears most often.

Another number that often is used to describe a set of data is the range. The **range** is the difference between the largest number and the smallest number in a set of data.

A **frequency table** shows how many times each piece of data occurs, usually in a survey. The frequency table below shows the results of a student survey on favorite color.

Color	Tally	Frequency
red	IIII	4
blue	HHI	5
black	II	2
green	III	3
purple	HHI II	7
yellow	HHI I	6

Based on the frequency table data, which color is the favorite?

Example The speeds (in m/s) for a race car during five different time trials are 39, 37, 44, 36, and 44.

To find the mean:
Step 1 Find the sum of the numbers.

$$39 + 37 + 44 + 36 + 44 = 200$$

Step 2 Divide the sum by the number of items, which is 5.

$$200 \div 5 = 40$$

The mean measure is 40 m/s.

To find the median:
Step 1 Arrange the measures from least to greatest.

$$36, \ 37, \ \underline{39}, \ 44, \ 44$$

Step 2 Determine the middle measure.

The median measure is 39 m/s.

To find the mode:
Step 1 Group the numbers that are the same together.

$$44, 44, 36, 37, 39$$

Step 2 Determine the number that occurs most in the set.

$$\underline{44, 44}, 36, 37, 39$$

The mode measure is 44 m/s.

To find the range:
Step 1 Arrange the measures from largest to smallest.

$$44, 44, 39, 37, 36$$

Step 2 Determine the largest and smallest measures in the set.

$$\underline{44}, 44, 39, 37, \underline{36}$$

Step 3 Find the difference between the largest and smallest measures.

$$44 - 36 = 8$$

The range is 8 m/s.

Practice Problem Find the mean, median, mode, and range for the data set 8, 4, 12, 8, 11, 14, 16.

Safety in the Science Classroom

1. Always obtain your teacher's permission to begin an investigation.

2. Study the procedure. If you have questions, ask your teacher. Be sure you understand any safety symbols shown on the page.

3. Use the safety equipment provided for you. Goggles and a safety apron should be worn during most investigations.

4. Always slant test tubes away from yourself and others when heating them or adding substances to them.

5. Never eat or drink in the lab, and never use lab glassware as food or drink containers. Never inhale chemicals. Do not taste any substances or draw any material into a tube with your mouth.

6. Report any spill, accident, or injury, no matter how small, immediately to your teacher, then follow his or her instructions.

7. Know the location and proper use of the fire extinguisher, safety shower, fire blanket, first aid kit, and fire alarm.

8. Keep all materials away from open flames. Tie back long hair and tie down loose clothing.

9. If your clothing should catch fire, smother it with the fire blanket, or get under a safety shower. NEVER RUN.

10. If a fire should occur, turn off the gas then leave the room according to established procedures.

Follow these procedures as you clean up your work area

1. Turn off the water and gas. Disconnect electrical devices.

2. Clean all pieces of equipment and return all materials to their proper places.

3. Dispose of chemicals and other materials as directed by your teacher. Place broken glass and solid substances in the proper containers. Make sure never to discard materials in the sink.

4. Clean your work area. Wash your hands thoroughly after working in the laboratory.

First Aid	
Injury	**Safe Response ALWAYS NOTIFY YOUR TEACHER IMMEDIATELY**
Burns	Apply cold water.
Cuts and Bruises	Stop any bleeding by applying direct pressure. Cover cuts with a clean dressing. Apply ice packs or cold compresses to bruises.
Fainting	Leave the person lying down. Loosen any tight clothing and keep crowds away.
Foreign Matter in Eye	Flush with plenty of water. Use eyewash bottle or fountain.
Poisoning	Note the suspected poisoning agent.
Any Spills on Skin	Flush with large amounts of water or use safety shower.

PERIODIC TABLE OF THE ELEMENTS

Columns of elements are called groups. Elements in the same group have similar chemical properties.

Element — Hydrogen
Atomic number — 1
Symbol — H
Atomic mass — 1.008
State of matter

Gas
Liquid
Solid
Synthetic

The first three symbols tell you the state of matter of the element at room temperature. The fourth symbol identifies human-made, or synthetic, elements.

1

1 | Hydrogen | 1 | **H** | 1.008

2 | Lithium | 3 | **Li** | 6.941 — Beryllium | 4 | **Be** | 9.012

3 | Sodium | 11 | **Na** | 22.990 — Magnesium | 12 | **Mg** | 24.305

	1	2	3	4	5	6	7	8	9
4	Potassium 19 **K** 39.098	Calcium 20 **Ca** 40.078	Scandium 21 **Sc** 44.956	Titanium 22 **Ti** 47.867	Vanadium 23 **V** 50.942	Chromium 24 **Cr** 51.996	Manganese 25 **Mn** 54.938	Iron 26 **Fe** 55.845	Cobalt 27 **Co** 58.933
5	Rubidium 37 **Rb** 85.468	Strontium 38 **Sr** 87.62	Yttrium 39 **Y** 88.906	Zirconium 40 **Zr** 91.224	Niobium 41 **Nb** 92.906	Molybdenum 42 **Mo** 95.94	Technetium 43 **Tc** (98)	Ruthenium 44 **Ru** 101.07	Rhodium 45 **Rh** 102.906
6	Cesium 55 **Cs** 132.905	Barium 56 **Ba** 137.327	Lanthanum 57 **La** 138.906	Hafnium 72 **Hf** 178.49	Tantalum 73 **Ta** 180.948	Tungsten 74 **W** 183.84	Rhenium 75 **Re** 186.207	Osmium 76 **Os** 190.23	Iridium 77 **Ir** 192.217
7	Francium 87 **Fr** (223)	Radium 88 **Ra** (226)	Actinium 89 **Ac** (227)	Rutherfordium 104 **Rf** (261)	Dubnium 105 **Db** (262)	Seaborgium 106 **Sg** (266)	Bohrium 107 **Bh** (264)	Hassium 108 **Hs** (277)	Meitnerium 109 **Mt** (268)

The number in parentheses is the mass number of the longest lived isotope for that element.

Rows of elements are called periods. Atomic number increases across a period.

The arrow shows where these elements would fit into the periodic table. They are moved to the bottom of the page to save space.

Lanthanide series	Cerium 58 **Ce** 140.116	Praseodymium 59 **Pr** 140.908	Neodymium 60 **Nd** 144.24	Promethium 61 **Pm** (145)	Samarium 62 **Sm** 150.36
Actinide series	Thorium 90 **Th** 232.038	Protactinium 91 **Pa** 231.036	Uranium 92 **U** 238.029	Neptunium 93 **Np** (237)	Plutonium 94 **Pu** (244)

SCIENCE Online
Visit the Glencoe Science
Web site at
science.glencoe.com
for updates to the periodic
table.

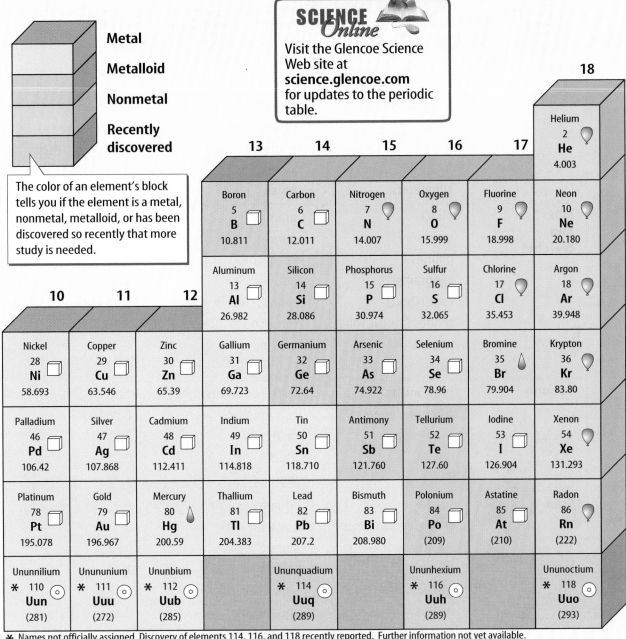

Metal

Metalloid

Nonmetal

Recently
discovered

The color of an element's block
tells you if the element is a metal,
nonmetal, metalloid, or has been
discovered so recently that more
study is needed.

	13	14	15	16	17	18
						Helium 2 He 4.003
	Boron 5 B 10.811	Carbon 6 C 12.011	Nitrogen 7 N 14.007	Oxygen 8 O 15.999	Fluorine 9 F 18.998	Neon 10 Ne 20.180
	Aluminum 13 Al 26.982	Silicon 14 Si 28.086	Phosphorus 15 P 30.974	Sulfur 16 S 32.065	Chlorine 17 Cl 35.453	Argon 18 Ar 39.948

10	11	12	13	14	15	16	17	18
Nickel 28 Ni 58.693	Copper 29 Cu 63.546	Zinc 30 Zn 65.39	Gallium 31 Ga 69.723	Germanium 32 Ge 72.64	Arsenic 33 As 74.922	Selenium 34 Se 78.96	Bromine 35 Br 79.904	Krypton 36 Kr 83.80
Palladium 46 Pd 106.42	Silver 47 Ag 107.868	Cadmium 48 Cd 112.411	Indium 49 In 114.818	Tin 50 Sn 118.710	Antimony 51 Sb 121.760	Tellurium 52 Te 127.60	Iodine 53 I 126.904	Xenon 54 Xe 131.293
Platinum 78 Pt 195.078	Gold 79 Au 196.967	Mercury 80 Hg 200.59	Thallium 81 Tl 204.383	Lead 82 Pb 207.2	Bismuth 83 Bi 208.980	Polonium 84 Po (209)	Astatine 85 At (210)	Radon 86 Rn (222)
Ununnilium * 110 Uun (281)	Unununium * 111 Uuu (272)	Ununbium * 112 Uub (285)		Ununquadium * 114 Uuq (289)		Ununhexium * 116 Uuh (289)		Ununoctium * 118 Uuo (293)

* Names not officially assigned. Discovery of elements 114, 116, and 118 recently reported. Further information not yet available.

Europium 63 Eu 151.964	Gadolinium 64 Gd 157.25	Terbium 65 Tb 158.925	Dysprosium 66 Dy 162.50	Holmium 67 Ho 164.930	Erbium 68 Er 167.259	Thulium 69 Tm 168.934	Ytterbium 70 Yb 173.04	Lutetium 71 Lu 174.967
Americium 95 Am (243)	Curium 96 Cm (247)	Berkelium 97 Bk (247)	Californium 98 Cf (251)	Einsteinium 99 Es (252)	Fermium 100 Fm (257)	Mendelevium 101 Md (258)	Nobelium 102 No (259)	Lawrencium 103 Lr (262)

Reference
Handbook

SI—Metric/English, English/Metric Conversions

	When you want to convert:	To:	Multiply by:
Length	inches	centimeters	2.54
	centimeters	inches	0.39
	yards	meters	0.91
	meters	yards	1.09
	miles	kilometers	1.61
	kilometers	miles	0.62
Mass and Weight*	ounces	grams	28.35
	grams	ounces	0.04
	pounds	kilograms	0.45
	kilograms	pounds	2.2
	tons (short)	tonnes (metric tons)	0.91
	tonnes (metric tons)	tons (short)	1.10
	pounds	newtons	4.45
	newtons	pounds	0.22
Volume	cubic inches	cubic centimeters	16.39
	cubic centimeters	cubic inches	0.06
	liters	quarts	1.06
	quarts	liters	0.95
	gallons	liters	3.78
Area	square inches	square centimeters	6.45
	square centimeters	square inches	0.16
	square yards	square meters	0.83
	square meters	square yards	1.19
	square miles	square kilometers	2.59
	square kilometers	square miles	0.39
	hectares	acres	2.47
	acres	hectares	0.40
Temperature	To convert °Celsius to °Fahrenheit		$°C \times 9/5 + 32$
	To convert °Fahrenheit to °Celsius		$5/9 \, (°F - 32)$

*Weight is measured in standard Earth gravity.

English Glossary

This glossary defines each key term that appears in bold type in the text. It also shows the chapter, section, and page number where you can find the words used.

A

alternating current (AC): electric current that changes its direction many times each second. (Chap. 2, Sec. 2, p. 50)

aurora: southern and northern lights that appear when charged particles trapped in the magnetosphere collide with Earth's atmosphere above the poles. (Chap. 2 Sec. 2, p. 49)

B

binary system: number system consisting of two digits (0 and 1) that can be used by devices, such as computers, to store or use information. (Chap. 3, Sec. 2, p. 74)

C

circuit: closed-conducting loop through which electric current can flow. (Chap. 1, Sec. 2, p. 15)

computer software: any list of instructions that a user gives to a computer. (Chap. 3, Sec. 2, p. 77)

conductor: material, such as copper or silver, through which electrons can move easily. (Chap. 1, Sec. 1, p. 12)

D

digital signal: electronic signal that does not vary smoothly with time, has only certain values, and can be represented by a series of numbers. (Chap. 3, Sec. 1, p. 67)

diode: semiconductor device that allows electric current to flow in only one direction and is commonly used to change alternating current to direct current. (Chap. 3, Sec. 1, p. 70)

direct current (DC): electric current that flows only in one direction. (Chap. 2, Sec. 2, p. 51)

E

electric current: flow of charge—either flowing electrons or flowing ions—through a conductor. (Chap. 1, Sec. 2, p. 15)

electric discharge: rapid movement of excess charge from one place to another. (Chap. 1, Sec. 1, p. 13)

electric field: field through which electric charges exert a force on each other. (Chap. 1, Sec. 1, p. 11)

electric force: attractive or repulsive force exerted by all charged objects on each other. (Chap. 1, Sec. 1, p. 11)

electric power: rate at which an electric appliance converts electrical energy into another form of energy; usage is measured by electric meters in kilowatt-hours. (Chap. 1, Sec. 3, p. 24)

electromagnet: magnet created by wrapping a current-carrying wire around an iron core. (Chap. 2, Sec. 2, p. 45)

electronic signal: a changing electric current that is used to carry information; can be analog or digital. (Chap. 3, Sec. 1, p. 66)

English Glossary

G

generator: device that uses a magnetic field to turn kinetic energy into electrical energy and can produce direct current and alternating current. (Chap. 2, Sec. 2, p. 50)

I

insulator: material, such as wood or glass, through which electrons cannot move easily. (Chap. 1, Sec. 1, p. 12)

integrated circuit: circuit that can contain millions of interconnected transistors and diodes imprinted on a tiny chip. (Chap. 3, Sec. 1, p. 71)

ion: a positively or negatively charged atom. (Chap. 1, Sec. 1, p. 8)

M

magnetic domain: group of atoms whose fields point in the same direction. (Chap. 2, Sec. 1, p. 40)

magnetic field: area surrounding a magnet through which magnetic force is exerted and that extends between a magnet's north and south poles. (Chap. 2, Sec. 1, p. 39)

magnetosphere: magnetic field surrounding Earth that deflects most of the charged particles flowing from the Sun. (Chap. 2, Sec. 1, p. 41)

microprocessor: integrated circuit that stores information, makes computations, and directs the computer's actions. (Chap. 3, Sec. 2, p. 79)

M (continued)

motor: device that transforms electrical energy into kinetic energy. (Chap. 2, Sec. 2, p. 48)

O

Ohm's law: relationship among voltage, current, and resistance in a circuit. (Chap. 1, Sec. 3, p. 21)

P

parallel circuit: circuit that has more than one path for electric current to follow. (Chap. 1, Sec. 3, p. 23)

R

random-access memory (RAM): temporary electronic memory within a computer. (Chap. 3, Sec. 2, p. 76)

read-only memory (ROM): electronic memory that is permanently stored within a computer. (Chap. 3, Sec. 2, p. 76)

resistance: a measure of how difficult it is for electrons to flow through a material; unit is the ohm (Ω). (Chap. 1, Sec. 2, p. 18)

S

semiconductor: element, such as silicon, whose electrical conductivity can be increased by adding impurities. (Chap. 3, Sec. 1, p. 69)

series circuit: circuit that has only one path for electric current to follow. (Chap. 1, Sec. 3, p. 22)

static charge: buildup of electric charge on an object. (Chap. 1, Sec. 1, p. 9)

T

transformer: device used to increase or decrease the voltage of an alternating current with little loss of energy. (Chap. 2, Sec. 2, p. 52)

transistor: semiconductor device that can amplify the strength of an electric signal or act as an electronic switch. (Chap. 3, Sec. 1, p. 71)

V

voltage: a measure of how much electrical energy each electron of a battery has; measured in volts (V). (Chap. 1, Sec. 2, p. 16)

Spanish Glossary

Este glossario define cada término clave que aparece en negrillas en el texto. También muestra el capítulo, la sección y el número de página en donde se usa dicho término.

A

alternating current (AC) / corriente alterna (CA): corriente eléctrica que cambia de dirección muchas veces cada segundo. (Cap. 2, Sec. 2, pág. 50)

aurora / aurora: luces boreales y australes que parecen cambiar cuando las partículas atrapadas en la magnetosfera chocan con la atmósfera de la Tierra por encima de los polos. (Cap. 2, Sec. 2, pág. 49)

B

binary system / sistema binario: sistema numérico que consta de dos dígitos, 0 y 1; se puede usar en dispositivos como las computadoras para almacenar o usar información. (Cap. 3, Sec. 2, pág. 74)

C

circuit / circuito: bucle conductor cerrado por donde puede fluir la corriente eléctrica. (Cap. 1, Sec. 2, pág. 15)

computer software / programa de computadora: cualquier lista de instrucciones que el usuario le da a la computadora. (Cap. 3, Sec. 2, pág. 77)

conductor / conductor: material, como el cobre o la plata, a través del cual los electrones se pueden desplazar fácilmente. (Cap. 1, Sec. 1, pág. 12)

D

digital signal / señal digital: señal electrónica que no varía suavemente con el tiempo, tiene sólo ciertos valores y se puede representar por una serie de números. (Cap. 3, Sec. 1, pág. 67)

diode / diodo: dispositivo semiconductor que permite que la corriente eléctrica fluya en una sola dirección; se usa comúnmente para convertir la corriente alterna en corriente directa. (Cap. 3, Sec. 1, pág. 70)

direct current (DC) / corriente directa (CD): corriente eléctrica que fluye en una sola dirección. (Cap. 2, Sec. 2, pág. 51)

E

electric current / corriente eléctrica: flujo de corriente, ya sea un flujo de electrones o de iones, a través de un conductor. (Cap. 1, Sec. 2, pág. 15)

electric discharge / descarga eléctrica: movimiento rápido del exceso de carga de un lugar a otro. (Cap. 1, Sec. 1, pág. 13)

electric field / campo eléctrico: campo a través del cual las cargas eléctricas ejercen una fuerza mutua. (Cap. 1, Sec. 1, pág. 11)

electric force / fuerza eléctrica: fuerza de atracción o de repulsión que ejercen todos los objetos con carga. (Cap. 1, Sec. 1, pág. 11)

electric power / potencia eléctrica: tasa a la cual un artefacto eléctrico convierte la energía eléctrica en otra forma de energía; su uso se mide en kilovatios-hora con contadores de electricidad. (Cap. 1, Sec. 3, pág. 24)

electromagnet / electroimán: imán creado al enrollar un alambre que conduce corriente alrededor de un núcleo de hierro. (Cap. 2, Sec. 2, pág. 45)

electronic signal / señal electrónica: una corriente eléctrica variable que se usa para transportar información; puede ser análoga o digital. (Cap. 3, Sec. 1, pág. 66)

G

generator / generador: dispositivo que utiliza un campo magnético para convertir la energía cinética en energía eléctrica y el cual produce corriente directa y corriente alterna. (Cap. 2, Sec. 2, pág. 50)

I

insulator / aislador: material a través del cual no pueden fluir los electrones fácilmente; por ejemplo, la madera o el vidrio. (Cap. 1, Sec. 1, pág. 12)

integrated circuit / circuito integrado: circuito que puede contener millones de transistores y diodos interconectados impresos en una pastilla diminuta. (Cap. 3, Sec. 1, pág. 71)

ion / ion: átomo con carga positiva o negativa. (Cap. 1, Sec. 1, pág. 8)

M

magnetic domain / dominio magnético: grupo de átomos cuyos campos magnéticos apuntan en la misma dirección. (Cap. 2, Sec. 1, pág. 40)

magnetic field / campo magnético: área que rodea un imán a través de la cual se ejerce la fuerza magnética y que se extiende entre el polo norte del imán y el polo sur. (Cap. 2, Sec. 1, pág. 39)

magnetosphere / magnetosfera: campo magnético que rodea la Tierra y el cual desvía la mayor parte de las partículas cargadas provenientes del Sol. (Cap. 2, Sec. 1, pág. 41)

microprocessor / microprocesador: circuito integrado que almacena información, hace cálculos y dirige las operaciones de una computadora. (Cap. 3, Sec. 2, pág. 79)

motor / motor: dispositivo que puede transformar la energía eléctrica en energía cinética. (Cap. 2, Sec. 2, pág. 48)

O

Ohm's law / ley de Ohm: relación entre el voltaje, la corriente y la resistencia en un circuito. (Cap. 1, Sec. 3, pág. 21)

P

parallel circuit / circuito paralelo: circuito que tiene más de una trayectoria para el flujo de la corriente eléctrica. (Cap. 1, Sec. 3, pág. 23)

Spanish Glossary

Spanish Glossary

R

random-access memory (RAM) / memoria de acceso directo (RAM): memoria electrónica temporal dentro de la computadora. (Cap. 3, Sec. 2, pág. 76)

read-only memory (ROM) / memoria de sólo lectura: memoria electrónica permanentemente almacenada en una computadora. (Cap. 3, Sec. 2, pág. 76)

resistance / resistencia: una medida del grado de dificultad con que los electrones pueden fluir a través de un material; la unidad de medida es el omnio (Ω). (Cap. 1, Sec. 2, pág. 18)

S

semiconductor / semiconductor: elemento como el silicio, cuya conductividad eléctrica puede aumentarse al añadirle impurezas. (Cap. 3, Sec. 1, pág. 69)

series circuit / circuito en serie: circuito con una sola trayectoria a través de la cual puede fluir la corriente eléctrica. (Cap. 1, Sec. 3, pág. 22)

static charge / carga estática: acumulación de cargas eléctricas en un objeto. (Cap. 1, Sec. 1, pág. 9)

T

transformer / transformador: dispositivo que se usa para aumentar o rebajar el voltaje de una corriente alterna y el cual produce poca pérdida de energía. (Cap. 2, Sec. 2, pág. 52)

transistor / transistor: dispositivo semiconductor que puede amplificar la fuerza de una señal eléctrica o actuar como un interruptor electrónico. (Cap. 3, Sec. 1, pág. 71)

V

voltage / voltaje: una medida de la cantidad de energía eléctrica que tiene cada electrón en una batería; se mide en voltios (V). (Cap. 1, Sec. 2, pág. 16)

The index for *Electricity and Magnetism* will help you locate major topics in the book quickly and easily. Each entry in the index is followed by the number of the pages on which the entry is discussed. A page number given in boldfaced type indicates the page on which that entry is defined. A page number given in italic type indicates a page on which the entry is used in an illustration or photograph. The abbreviation *act.* indicates a page on which the entry is used in an activity.

Index

Credits

Art Credits

Glencoe would like to acknowledge the artists and agencies who participated in illustrating this program: Absolute Science Illustration; Andrew Evansen; Argosy; Articulate Graphics; Craig Attebery represented by Frank & Jeff Lavaty; CHK America; Gagliano Graphics; Pedro Julio Gonzalez represented by Melissa Turk & The Artist Network; Robert Hynes represented by Mendola Ltd.; Morgan Cain & Associates; JTH Illustration; Laurie O'Keefe; Matthew Pippin represented by Beranbaum Artist's Representative; Precision Graphics; Publisher's Art; Rolin Graphics, Inc.; Wendy Smith represented by Melissa Turk & The Artist Network; Kevin Torline represented by Berendsen and Associates, Inc.; WILDlife ART; Phil Wilson represented by Cliff Knecht Artist Representative; Zoo Botanica.

Photo Credits

Abbreviation key: AA=Animals Animals; AH=Aaron Haupt; AMP=Amanita Pictures; BC=Bruce Coleman, Inc.; CB=CORBIS; DM=Doug Martin; DRK=DRK Photo; ES=Earth Scenes; FP=Fundamental Photographs; GH=Grant Heilman Photography; IC=Icon Images; KS=KS Studios; LA=Liaison Agency; MB=Mark Burnett; MM=Matt Meadows; PE=PhotoEdit; PD=PhotoDisc; PQ=PictureQuest; PR=Photo Researchers; SB=Stock Boston; TSA=Tom Stack & Associates; TSM=The Stock Market; VU=Visuals Unlimited.

Cover PD; **iv** Peter Menzel/SB/PQ; **v** John Evans; **vi** Richard Megna/FP; **1** (l)Digital Vision/PQ, (r)Richard Hutchings; **2** (t)CB, (b)SuperStock; **3** Ace Photo Agency/PhotoTake NYC; **4** Lester Lefkowitz/TSM; **5** (t)AP/Wide World Photos, (b)PD; **6** AH; **6-7** Peter Menzel/SB/PQ; **7** Geoff Butler; **9** (t)Richard Hutchings, (b)KS; **10** Stephen R. Wagner; **14** J. Tinning/PR; **22** DM; **23** (t)DM, (b)Geoff Butler; **25** Bonnie Freer/PR; **27** (t)Brown Brothers, (b)MM; **28 29** Richard Hutchings; **30-31** Tom & Pat Leeson/PR; **31** William Munoz/PR; **32** (t)DM, (c)Matt York/AP/Wide World Photos, (b)IC; **34** DM; **36** John Evans; **36-37** Argus Fotoarchiv/Peter Arnold, Inc.; **37** MM; **39** Richard Megna/FP; **40** AMP; **42** PD; **43** John Evans; **45** (l)Kodansha, (c)Manfred Kage/Peter Arnold, Inc., (r)DM; **49** Bjorn Backe Papilio/CB; **51** Norbert Schafer/TSM; **53** AT&T Bell Labs/Science Photo Library/PR; **56** (tl)Science Photo Library/PR, (tr)Fermilab/Science Photo Library/PR, (b)SuperStock; **57** PD; **58** (t)file photo, (b)AH; **59** AH; **60** (tl)IC, (tr)Digital Vision/PQ, (bl)StockTrek/PD, (br)Spencer Grant/PE; **61** (l)SIU/Peter Arnold, Inc., (r)Latent Image; **62** file photo; **64-65** Adam Hart-Davis/Science Photo Library/PR; **65** (t)Dale E. Boyer/PR, (b)John Evans; **66** Willie L. Hill, Jr./SB; **67** (l)IC, (r)DM; **69** (l)CMCD/PD, (c)Russ Lappa, (r)CMCD/PD; **70** AMP; **71** (t)AMP, (b)Charles Falco/PR; **72** Charles Falco/PR; **73** (l)Bettmann/CB, (r)IC; **76** (l)courtesy IBM/Florida State University, (r)Andrew Syred/Science Photo Library/PR; **77** MB; **79** file photo; **80** Thomas Brummett/PD; **81** Slim Films; **82** (l)Dr. Dennis Kunkel/PhotoTake NYC, (r)AH; **83** Timothy Fuller; **84** (t)Frank Cezus, (b)John Evans; **85** John Evans; **87** (l)David York/The Stock Shop, (r)Tek Images/Science Photo Library/PR; **88** (t)MB, (c)Russell Illig/PD, (b)AH; **89** (tl)Keith Brofsky/PD, (tr)AMP, (b)AH; **94-95** PD; **96** CB; **97** (t)John Dudak/PhotoTake NYC/PQ, (b)Bill Vaine/CB; **98** (t)NOAA Photo Library/Central Library, OAR/ERL/National Severe Storms Laboratory (NSSL), (c)Richard Hamilton Smith/CB, (b)Jeffry W. Myers/CB; **99** Geophysical Institute, University of Alaska Fairbanks via RE/MAX/AP/Wide World Photos; **100** Timothy Fuller; **104** Roger Ball/TSM; **106** (l)Geoff Butler, (r)Coco McCoy/Rainbow/PQ; **107** Dominic Oldershaw; **108** StudiOhio; **109** First Image; **111** MM; **114** Paul Barton/TSM; **117** Davis Barber/PE.